A Step-by-Step Guide to
Woven Carpets and Rugs

by Ann Croot

HAMLYN

London · New York · Sydney · Toronto

Acknowledgements

I would like to thank the following for allowing me to use photographs of their rugs and samplers, and for their help and kindness to me while I was preparing this book; Mary Bennett, Susan Bridge, Peter Collingwood, Craftsman's Mark Limited, Martin Griffiths, Lorraine Hughes, Neil Ireson, Gwen Mullins, Roger Oates, Tony Pugh, Peter Sparkes, Helen Turgoose.

Also the following students of the College of Art, Stourbridge, Worcestershire; Helen Broadsmith, Ann Curry, Robert Holmes, Giles Horner, Sarah Surman.

Published by
The Hamlyn Publishing Group Ltd
London · New York · Sydney · Toronto
Astronaut House, Feltham, Middlesex, England
© Copyright The Hamlyn Publishing Group Ltd 1974
ISBN 0 600 38069 6

Printed in England by
Chapel River Press (IPC Printers),
Andover, Hampshire.

Contents

Contents continued

Glossary of terms

Batten. The heavy bar attached to the loom with which the weft is beaten into place.

Cross. The cross made in the warp threads during winding to keep the ends in order.

Finger hank. Wound hank of yarn that unwinds from the centre.

Heading. The strip of weft at each end of the rug between the fringe and the rug itself.

Heddle. Knotted string specially made to lift individual warp ends, or a metal strip, or wire with a loop or eye in the centre suspended between shaft sticks.

Leashes. Lengths of string or cord, individually looped under the opposite warp ends (those not raised by the shed stick). Leashes are tied in bunches, so that when lifted they raise the warp to make the second shed.

Loom. The frame or machine on which weaving is done.

Raddle. A square section stick with nails or pegs in it at regular intervals, used for spacing the warp.

Rug fork. A heavy pronged fork used to beat down the weft when there is no batten on the loom.

Selvedge. The group of reinforced warp ends at each side of the rug.

Shaft. The frame on which groups of heddles are tied.

Shed. The V-shaped space between raised and lowered warp ends, through which the weft pick passes.

Shed stick. The wooden stick which, when turned on its side in the warp, raises one set of alternate warp ends, thus making a shed.

Shuttle. The container on which the weft is wound.

Tenterhook. An expanding gauge used to keep the width of the rug constant.

Warp. The threads held taut lengthwise in the loom, and through which the weft threads are woven to make fabric.

Warp ends. Individual lengths of warp thread, sometimes referred to simply as 'ends'.

Warping board. Board with spaced pegs on which the warp is wound.

Warping peg. An individual peg which can be clamped on to a suitable surface to help make a warp.

Weft. The threads interwoven at right-angles with the warp threads.

Weft picks. Individual weft threads.

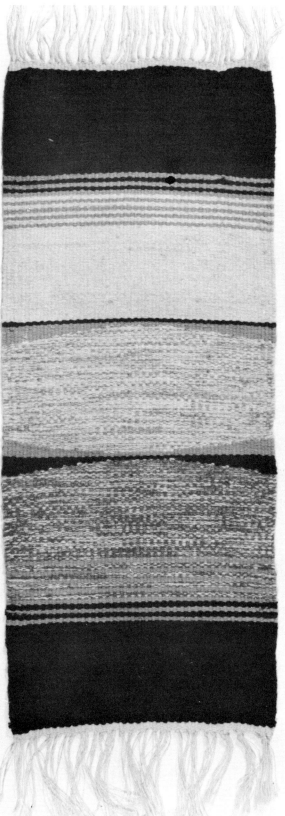

Sampler in tapestry weave showing gradation in tone
Gwen Mullins

Sampler in bands and ovals in kilim technique
Gwen Mullins

Introduction

Weaving rugs and carpets for your home or for special gifts is a fascinating and rewarding craft and one which anyone can master with a little patience and a great deal of practise. Even if you have never tried weaving before, by working through this book, step by step, you will be able to master the basic principles of weaving and learn enough to be able to make beautiful wall hangings, rugs and carpets.

Perhaps you are not sure that you want to invest in a loom at this stage. On page 9, you are shown how a simple frame loom can be made from strips of wood, at home, or from an old iron bedstead, or even tubular scaffolding. A loom, in its simplest form, is a very straightforward structure and some of the most exquisite fabrics woven by primitive peoples were produced on looms similar to the ones described.

In the final section of this book, you will find some simple rug designs which I hope you will try, using the techniques I have explained. In fact, all the beautiful examples which illustrate this book can be worked with the same techniques. You might start by making a sampler, but keep a notebook by you as you work. You may chance on an exciting effect accidentally and it is always difficult to remember later exactly how something was done.

There are endless possibilities to try, using colours and shapes, and soon you will be making your first rug. Perhaps, when you have experienced the deep satisfaction and the sense of pleasure and achievement that weaving brings, you will want to progress to one of the larger looms which are available – and to the greater excitement they can provide.

Ann Croot
Stourbridge College of Art.

Sampler on a frame *Lorraine Hughes*

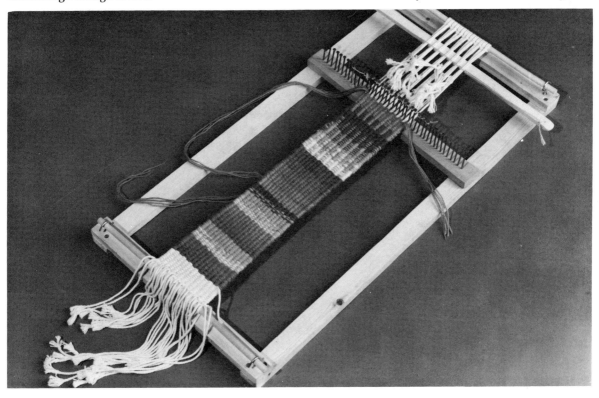

The process called weaving

Weaving, in its simplest definition, is the interlacing of two sets of threads at right angles to each other, to produce a fabric. The lengthwise or vertical threads, those held on the loom, are called the warp and individual warp threads are called 'ends'. The threads which are interlaced horizontally are called the weft and one row of weft is called a 'pick'. To make it possible to interlace the weft threads easily, the warp threads are put on the loom and held at even tension. Most of us know what ordinary darning looks like and the way in which the darning needle is worked – over a thread, under a thread. This is rather how plain weaving is worked but instead of a needle, a shuttle is used to carry the weft yarn.

In darning, all the lengthwise or warp threads lie side by side and the needle is threaded through. In plain weaving, every other warp thread is lifted by a device (depending on the kind of loom), thus forming a triangular space for the shuttle to pass through. This space is called a 'shed' and frame looms have two.

The loom

Fig. 1: *The construction of a simple frame loom (see also* Fig. 5b).
Fig. 2: *The raddle, a shed stick and a shuttle.*

The loom is the frame or machine on which the warp is held at tension. There are four basic types – the frame loom, the upright or vertical loom, the table loom and the floor loom. Upright or vertical looms are traditionally used for weaving rugs.

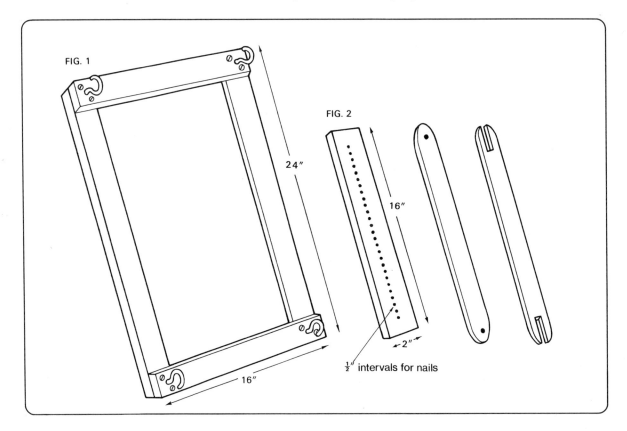

FIG. 1

24"

16"

FIG. 2

16"

2"

½" intervals for nails

Constructing a frame loom

The instructions are for a frame 24in by 16in, which will be large enough to weave samples.

You will need a length of planed timber, 10ft by 2in by 1in; a length of planed timber 4ft 6in by 1in by $\frac{1}{4}$in; 3ft of dowelling rod or metal rod, $\frac{1}{2}$in thick; 4 brass $1\frac{1}{2}$in hooks; 8 by $1\frac{1}{4}$in No. 6 screws, and $\frac{1}{2}$lb $2\frac{1}{2}$in round-head nails.

From the 2in by 1in timber, cut three lengths, each 16in long, and two lengths, each 24in long; from the 1in by $\frac{1}{4}$in timber cut three lengths, each 18in.

Make the frame by laying two 16in lengths across the two 24in lengths, making sure the corners are square, and screwing them together with two screws in each corner, Figs. 1 and 2. Screw a hook into each corner so that the open end of the hooks face outwards. Cut the metal or wooden dowelling rod in half to make the rod on which the warp is tied. These rods are held in position by the hooks, Fig 5b.

The raddle is made by embedding nails at intervals of 2/5in along the centre line of the remaining 16in length of wood: $\frac{1}{8}$in holes must be drilled approximately $\frac{1}{4}$in deep and the nails tapped into position because if they are hammered home, the wood will split.

To make the shed sticks, round off and smooth the ends of two of the 18in pieces of wood and drill an $\frac{1}{8}$in hole 1in from each end.

To make a wooden shuttle cut slots 1in deep and $\frac{1}{4}$in wide in each end of the remaining 18in length of wood, and smooth off the rough surfaces.

Adjustable frame looms

One of the earliest types of horizontal loom consisted of two horizontal sticks round which the warp was wound in a figure eight (Fig. 3). The purpose of the figure eight method of winding is to keep the warp ends in order. The two sticks were attached to four corner pegs driven into the ground by means of a slip knot. This principle could be adapted using an old bedstead or a large picture frame, warp bars being tied to the top and bottom of the frame with slip knots (Fig. 4). The tension of the warp is adjusted by tightening the slip knots.

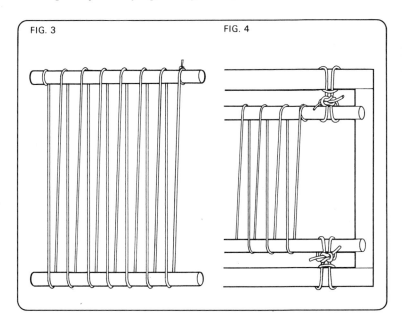

Fig. 3: *Winding the warp on to two warp bars in a figure of eight.*
Fig. 4: *Attaching the bars to a frame by means of slip knots.*

Rigid warp looms are available commercially with a built-in raddle but a home-made version can be made from pieces of wood, from an artist's stretcher, from a picture frame or from an iron bedstead, (Fig. 5a, 5b).

As we have said, some of the most beautiful examples of fabrics produced by primitive people were woven on such looms.

Adjustable frame looms can be purchased and are available in various sizes. On these, the woven fabric is pushed round to the back of the loom and the length of the finished rug or sample is thus limited to twice the length of the frame.

Another type of frame loom available commercially has one fixed warp bar and one that can be tightened as the weaving progresses (Fig. 6). These are suitable for weaving both samplers and rugs. A similar type of loom could be constructed at home in wood or adapted from alloy scaffolding tubing (Fig. 7).

Fig. 5: (a) *and* (b): *Two types of rigid frame looms.*
Fig. 6: *Adjustable wooden frame* (a) *with notched warp bar and* (b) *with nailed raddle to space the warp.*
Fig. 7: *Adjustable frame loom made of scaffolding.*

10

The scaffolding loom

To make a loom from tubular scaffolding, you need alloy tubing with galvanised joints, two lengths of cast-iron screw with two wing nuts on each length, and two lengths of screw, each with a foot and one wing nut. Four brackets are also needed to fix the frame to the wall so that the frame does not fall over. The top pair are screwed tightly to the frame and the bottom pair fix the lower part of the frame to the wall but allow the tubing to move down through them when the top and bottom bars are being adjusted.

The tension is adjusted by making the space between the top pair of wing nuts greater and at the same time making the space between the foot and the bottom wing nut smaller. By doing this, the distance between the top and bottom warp bars is increased, and the warp tightened.

The vertical rug loom with two sets of shafts or frames to hold the heddles, and two rollers for winding on the warp, is a more sophisticated version of these looms, with mechanical aids to make weaving faster, but the principal of working is the same (Fig. 8).

You have now made, or purchased, a loom. The next step is to get it ready for weaving.

The shed

The shed is the triangular space made between one set of raised warp ends and the other lowered ends through which the weft passes (Fig. 9).

To weave plain weave, or Tabby weave as it is sometimes called, the even numbered ends are lifted first, thus making the first shed, and then the odd numbered ends are lifted, making the second shed.

Fig. 8: *Two-frame loom.*

Fig. 9: (a): *Making the first shed with a shed stick;* (b): *Making the second shed by lifting the leashes.*

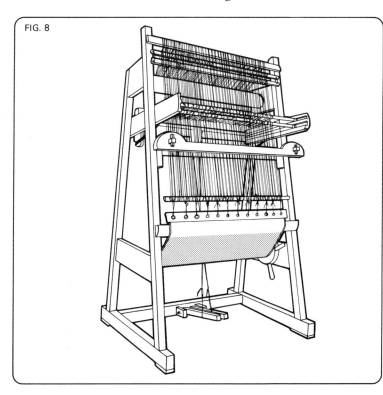

FIG. 8

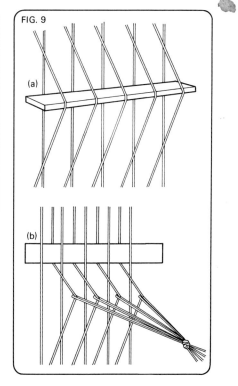

FIG. 9

(a)

(b)

On frame looms, the two sheds are made very simply by using a shed stick for the first shed and groups of leashes for the second shed.

To make the first shed, thread the stick across the warp from the right under the odd numbered ends.

This stick should always be longer than the width of the warp and about 2in wide. The shed is made by turning the stick on its side.

For the second shed, leashes are made as follows: Cut pieces of thick string 9in long. You cut half the total number of warp ends. Tie each piece of string individually round each of the warp ends lying under the shed stick. Knot the ends together in an overhand knot. Knot the leashes together in groups of four across the warp.

The second shed is made by lifting these groups of leashes in turn and passing the weft through the V-shaped space. In this way, the shed stick lifts even-numbered ends, and the leashes lift odd-numbered ends.

In the 2-frame vertical rug looms, one heddle frame is threaded with odd-numbered ends, and the other frame threaded with even-numbered ends, and the two sheds made by pulling first one frame forward and then the other (Fig. 10).

Fig. 10: How the shed is made on a two-frame rug loom.

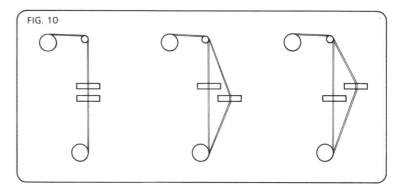

FIG. 10

Warping

Fig. 11: (a): Attaching the warp to a rigid frame loom; (b): Attaching the warp to a home-made frame loom.

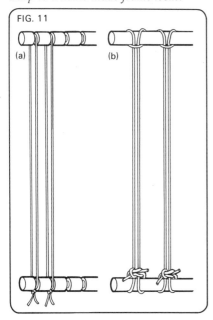

FIG. 11

(a)   (b)

The warp must be tied as taut as possible and the threads must lie parallel with each other so that the weft can pass over and under them with ease. The way in which the warp is attached to the loom varies according to the construction of the loom.

Warping the rigid frame loom
Each length of warp yarn makes two warp ends as it is looped at the top of the frame and tied at the bottom. The required number of lengths is therefore half the number of warp ends (Fig. 11).

The length of each piece of warp yarn is twice the height of the frame, plus twice the length of the intended fringe and the amount needed to tie the knot on the bottom of the frame.

In the rigid frame type of loom with grooved bars, the warp thread lies in a groove at the top of the frame, is brought down and is tied in a reef knot under the lower grooved warp bar (Fig. 11a).

In the home-made frame loom, both ends of warp yarn are looped over the top bar, brought down over the bottom bar and taken to the back, each end then being brought out at each side to the front, and tying the ends in a single knot (Fig. 11b). The tension is adjusted by pulling the two ends firmly upwards, and completing the reef knot, or making a half bow.

Warping the adjustable frame loom

The warp yarn is first wound into a ball. Tie the end of the yarn temporarily to the bottom bar. Wind it up and over the top and under the bottom bars continuously, until the required width of warp is achieved. Finish winding at the bottom bar. Cut the end of the yarn and tie it to the previous warp end on the bottom bar. Undo the beginning knot and tie it to the next warp end on the bottom bar.

The warp tied in this way is continuous, so that the weaving can be moved round on the frame. The weaving is done on the threads at the front of the loom, and so by moving the warp round as weaving proceeds, it is possible to weave a rug almost twice the length of the frame (Fig. 12).

When counting the number of warp ends, remember to count only those lying on the front of the loom – the ones lying at the back must not be counted in.

Warping the two-frame rug loom

This type of loom is designed to hold enough warp for one or more rugs at one time and as there is always a certain amount of warp wastage in cutting a rug from a loom, it is obviously economic to put on more than one warp at a time.

There are several ways that a long warp can be made, but the principle is the same for all methods. First, work out the overall length of the warp – the method for doing this is on page 26. The warp, which is usually on a spool or in a skein, is then wound on a device of some kind so that all the threads are of the same length.

Two crosses are wound in the warp to keep the threads in order and to help in their easy separation when transferring them to the loom. You must be able to count the number of 'ends'.

Making a warp

The simplest equipment available for the purpose is a set of warp pegs which are fixed to a table with clamps (Fig. 13). Two of the pegs are fixed at each end of a measured distance, and the yarn is wound between them, thus making a cross (Fig. 14). The function of the crosses is to keep the warp threads in order until they are all safely on the loom.

The warp is tied to the first clamp at one end, A, (Fig. 14), taken outside B to the other end, goes between C and D, round D, between C and D again, back to the other end on the outside of B and between A and B. It is then taken round A, between A and B again and so to the other end. Winding in this way continues until the required number of warps has been wound round the pegs, finishing at A. Every time the yarn reaches point A, an even number of threads has been wound.

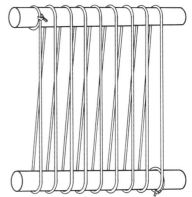

Fig. 12: Winding a continuous warp for the adjustable frame loom.

FIG. 12

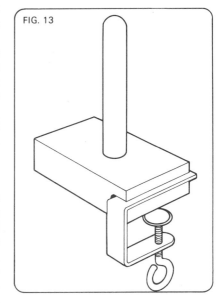

FIG. 13

Fig. 13: Warping peg with table clamp.

Fig. 14: Winding a warp using pegs clamped to a table.

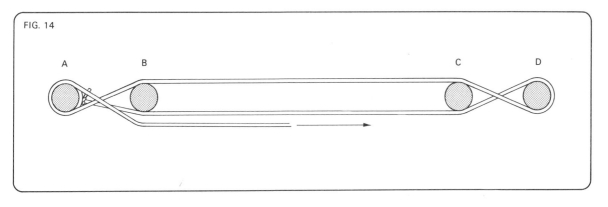

FIG. 14

To count the number of ends wound, loop a length of yarn around groups of threads while the winding is taking place (Fig. 15). This is done at one side of the warp so that, if there are four ends per inch, each group of four equals 2in.

The pegs method is not suitable for making a long warp; the pegs would have to be set so far apart that they would be unstable.

For long warps, a rectangular warping frame is the most convenient to use (Fig. 16). This is a frame with pegs at set intervals and the cross is wound at each end. The length of the warp is adjusted by winding around all or some of the pegs.

A warping mill is also used by weavers and this is the quickest and best way of winding a warp, but it is a bulky piece of equipment, needing a lot of space. The mill is an upright box frame that spins on a central pivot, and has adjustable positions for the pegs to make the crosses.

Tying the cross. The cross must be firmly and securely tied before the warp is removed from the warping frame. This can be done in two ways. Tie a length of ribbon around the cross (Fig. 17a), making sure that the cross is lying correctly and that the ribbon is securely tied. Alternatively, tie the warp firmly with ribbon in four areas near to the cross (Fig. 17b). It does no harm if beginners tie crosses in both ways.

Fig. 15: *Counting the number of ends wound in the warp.*

Fig. 16: *Warping frame with warp in position.*

Figs. 17a and b: *Two ways of tying the cross.*

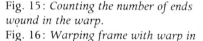

FIG. 15

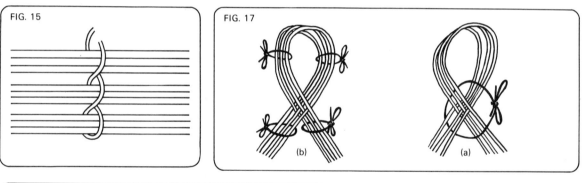

FIG. 17

(b) (a)

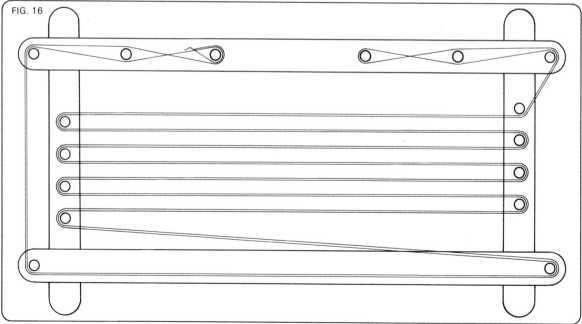

FIG. 16

Chaining the warp. The warp is next removed from the warping frame by chaining it (Fig. 18). This prevents it getting damaged and keeps the ends in order. To do this, hold the warp in the left hand and slip it from the starting pegs (A and B in Fig. 14).

Put the right hand over the top of the warp and pass it under the warp, pulling it gently towards you, having made a loop in the warp. Grasp the warp in the right hand as if you were shaking hands with it, and pull the warp through the first loop. Slip the hand through this loop and grasp the warp again; pull the warp through the loop again. Go on chaining this way until the cross at the other end of the pegged warp is reached. Slip the warp off the pegs CD. The warp is now ready to be wound on to the loom.

Fig. 18: *Five stages of chaining the warp.*

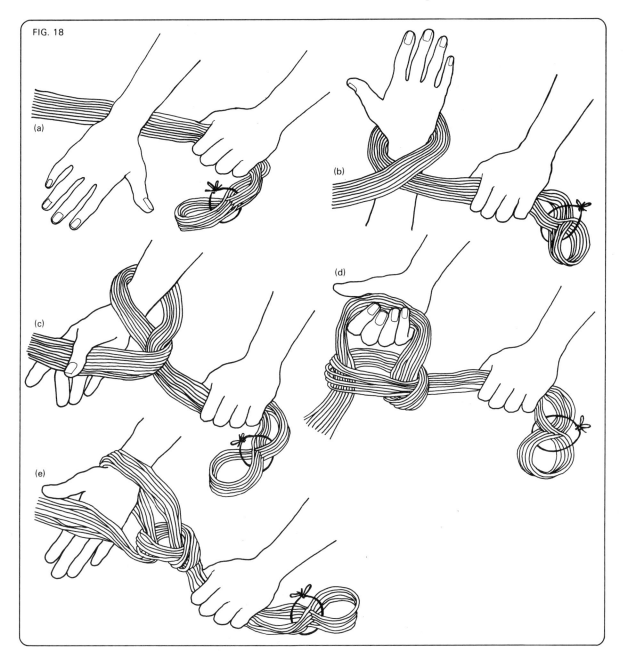

FIG. 18

(a)

(b)

(c)

(d)

(e)

The sett

The number of working warp ends to the inch is called, in weaving terminology, the sett. To decide how many warp ends will be put on the loom, you must first decide how wide the rug is to be and how dense.

If the warp threads are too thin for the weft, the rug will be rather sloppy and you will be able to poke your finger through it easily. If the warp is too thick for the weft, the finished rug will be rather stiff and hard and the weft will not be able to cover the warp properly.

The aim is, of course, to make a firm rug of good texture. This is done by adjusting the balance between the amount of warp ends per inch and the amount of weft per inch.

If a thick warp yarn is available it can be used singly, but it is more usual to use two, three or four warp threads together as one working warp end. It is usual to have between three and six working ends per inch in the warp. In general, the thicker the working ends per inch or the greater their number, the thinner the weft yarn must be.

The selvedge

During weaving, the outside warp ends get quite a lot of wear and therefore need to be strengthened. The area of strengthening is called the selvedge. In rug weaving, this area is particularly necessary because the rug edges are naturally given a lot of wear and tear in use.

To make a selvedge on a narrow rug, the two outside warp ends are worked together. In a wider rug, the four outside warp ends are worked together.

Preparing the weft

Once the warp is ready on the loom it remains only to prepare the weft so that you can start weaving. The weft yarn, which you will have purchased either on a spool or in a skein, has to be transferred to a shuttle of some kind. There are different types and sizes of shuttles and the one used depends both on the type of loom and the design of the rug.

Shuttles

Stick shuttle. The instructions for the home-constructed loom on page 9 include the making of a stick shuttle and this can be made to any length – ideally a shuttle should be at least 4in longer than the width of the weaving. Stick shuttles are used when the shed opening is narrow – such as on frame looms.

To fill a stick shuttle the wool is wound around one prong and then around the whole shuttle. It should not be overfilled or it will not pass easily through the shed (Fig. 21).

Fig. 21: The stick shuttle.

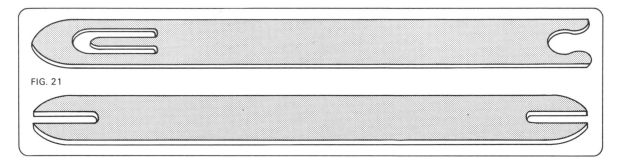

FIG. 21

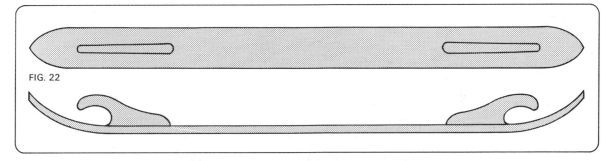

FIG. 22

Long rug shuttle. The long rug weaving shuttle is used when the rug is to be woven in a plain colour in broad stripes extending the full width of the warp. This shuttle is 34in long and is wide enough to take a generous amount of wool, leaving the pointed end free to slide easily through the warp (Fig. 22). The wool is wound across the open end, around the inner prong, returning down the same side.

Small shuttle. This type of shuttle is used when a number of different colours are being used in weaving. The shuttles can be left hanging without becoming unwound, and are a convenient size for weaving small blocks of colour. The pointed end of the shuttle is designed for beating down the weft (Fig. 23).

The wool is wound on the small shuttle as follows: with the wool on the right-hand side of the shuttle hanging point down, place the first finger of the right hand behind the wool, twist the finger downwards over it, picking up a loop, and slip this off the finger over the shuttle. Continue in this way until the shuttle is full; the wool will unwind freely as required.

Finger hank. On frame looms particularly, a finger hank can be used instead of a shuttle. This is made by winding the wool on the hand in a figure eight (Fig. 24a, b, c). They unwind easily from the centre. Finger hanks are sometimes used in making pile rugs as they are flexible and easy to work around a pile gauge.

Fig. 22: *The ski shuttle.*
Fig. 23: *Small shuttle for weaving blocks of colour.*
Fig. 24: *Three stages in making a finger hank.*

FIG. 23

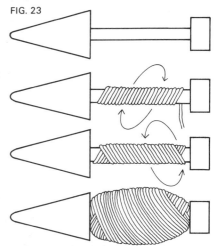

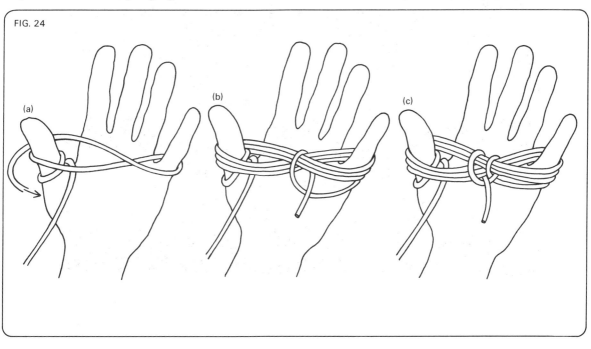

FIG. 24

(a)   (b)   (c)

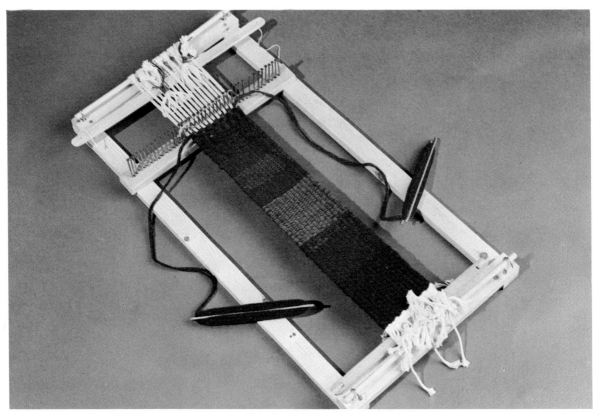

Detail of colour sample to show how bands can be broken up by
using varied amounts of each colour in the weft *Anne Curry*

Kilim band pattern *Gwen Mullins*

Hanging Rug *Tony Pugh*

Other weaving equipment

Skein winder and spool rack

Weaving yarn is sold either in skeins or wound on to large bobbins. It is necessary to be able to wind from these on to the shuttle easily and for this, a skein winder or a spool rack is used. The skein winder is collapsible and something like an umbrella frame. It can be fixed to a table and adjusts upwards to hold the skein (Fig. 25). A spool rack is a wooden frame with a number of movable metal bars on which spools are placed so that they unwind freely (Fig. 26).

Fig. 25: *Collapsible skein winder.*
Fig. 26: *A spool rack.*
Fig. 28: *A metal beater.*

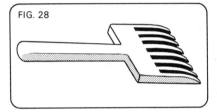

Tenterhook

A tenterhook is an adjustable wooden gauge with small metal teeth at each end. The tenterhook is used to check that the width of the rug is being kept constant but it is better to learn to weave without a tenterhook gauge (Fig. 27).

Beater

Frame looms do not have a batten to beat the weaving down into place and so this must be done using a beater. This is a large heavy metal fork, which is held in the hand, the prongs fitting between the warp ends. The weft is pushed down on every row of weaving so that it covers the warp completely (Fig. 28).

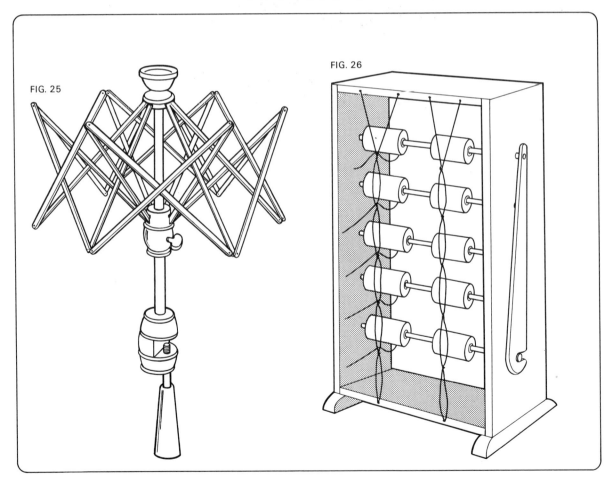

Yarns and materials

Weavers regard yarns, their raw materials, as a source of inspiration. The feel of them – as well as the appearance – can lead a weaver to experiment in both colours and textures and most of us feel that there could never be enough time to try out every combination of yarn. The creative possibilities in weaving are endless but in rug weaving there is a certain limitation in the choice of warp. Although almost any yarns can be used for the weft, the warp in rug weaving must be exceptionally strong.

Weft-face and plain weave rugs

In a weft-face rug the warp is completely covered by the weft and shows only at the ends in the fringes. As it is covered the warp yarn does not affect the appearance of the finished rug, but it does influence the handling and the way the rug lies on the floor. The best warp yarns for these rugs are cotton, wool, linen, hemp, jute, ramie and some synthetics. All of these are obtainable from weavers' suppliers.

A cotton yarn warp is good for beginners to use as it is easy to control, but when you have gained a little experience, try one of the cotton twines like those used in the fishing industry. These are more tightly spun and are quite elastic. The elasticity of cotton yarns is particularly helpful to beginners because, even if the warp isn't perfectly made, it will still weave satisfactorily. Cotton yarn is also easy to dye if a coloured fringe is preferred to the natural white.

Linen, hemp and ramie yarns are smooth and glossy and the wool weft slips easily down on the warp. They provide firmness and have a natural, pleasant colour which looks good as a fringe. Linen has little elasticity and the warp must therefore be perfectly made.

Weft yarns

Wool is the weft yarn most used in rug weaving, and it gives a good hardwearing surface. Choose a worsted spun yarn with medium twist and of fairly coarse fibres.

The 2-ply rug wool used in the carpet trade is suitable for weaving rugs and can be obtained, in a large range of colours, direct from carpet makers. The same yarn is made up into 6-ply specifically for rug weaving and can be bought from weavers' supply houses.

Fig. 27: *Two kinds of tenterhook.*

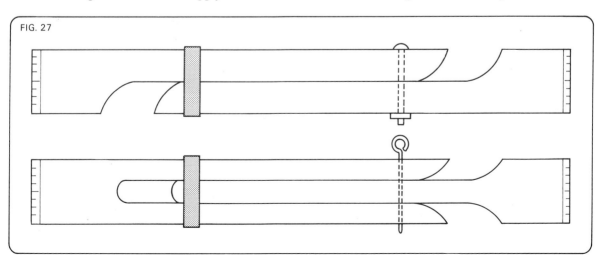

FIG. 27

Pink, white and silver *Roger Oates*

Shiraz Kilim, Persian 19th century, woven in wool and hair with
some of the white areas in cotton *Hamlyn Picture Library*

Pile yarn

Scandinavian suppliers produce special yarns for knotting, called rya and flossa yarns. These are a mixture yarn and do not shed their fibres as much as an ordinary woollen yarn when used for the same purpose.

Working out quantities

Sometimes, it is difficult to obtain warp yarn of sufficient weight and a finer thread has to be used, doubled, threefold or sometimes even four-fold. Ideally, rug warp should be at least 4-ply.

To calculate the quantity of warp yarn required for a rug, multiply the number of ends per inch (usually between four and six) by the width of the rug, which will give you the number of warp ends.

Multiply the number of warp ends by the length of the warp – this is the finished length of the rug, plus any wastage taken up on the loom. This will give you the entire warp length needed. Divide this number by the number of yards per pound in the chosen warp yarn, and you will arrive at the correct weight of yarn. The yards per pound are usually marked on the packet.

The weft poundage is calculated in a similar way. Work a small sample of weaving on a warped frame loom and multiply the number of weft threads per inch by the length of the rug. Allowance also has to be made for the yarn to curve over and under the warp threads – this is called the 'take-up'.

As an approximate guide: $\frac{1}{2}$ lb wool will work 1 sq ft of rug. Weft thread is supplied either in singles, 2-ply or 6-ply.

Sampler showing spots, lines in pick and pick, blocks tufting, looping
Helen Turgoose

Beginning weaving

So now you are ready to begin weaving. You have either made the non-adjustable frame loom or perhaps a simple adjustable loom from scaffolding. Or you may have purchased a vertical 2-frame loom. You have dressed the loom and prepared the weft. In this section you are shown how to achieve different patterns on your loom.

The heading

The heading is the name given to the band of weaving which lies between the fringe and the main part of the rug. It varies in depth between 1½in and 4in, depending on the design of the rug – shorter if the rug has a flat surface and longer if it is tufted. The heading has a dual purpose – to set the warp threads into position and make a firm base to weave against.

The heading is usually woven using the same yarn as for the warp, and this helps to soften the visual effect of the rug edge between the woven wool and the fringe.

Put a stick – a spare shed stick will do – through the shed made by the leashes and push it firmly into position against the bottom bar on the loom, to spread the warp correctly. This must be done or there will be warp wastage because of the gaps caused by the groups of tied warp threads.

Tie the stick to the bottom bar to stop the warp slipping. If a loom with a continuous warp is being used, this tie will have to be adjusted when the weaving is wound on later, and then retied.

Weaving the heading

Fill a shuttle with warp thread. The drawing of the frame loom on page 11 shows the stick pushed down into position and the shed stick turned on its side, ready to make the first shed. Pass the shuttle through the shed, across the warp, leaving the weft lying in an arc. Beat the centre of this arc down against the stick, then beat the centre of the arcs on either side of it into place, and so on until the weft is evenly in place, covering alternate warp threads (Fig. 29).

Push the shed stick up the loom. Make the second shed by pulling up each group of leashes in turn and passing the shuttle back through. Leave the weft yarn in an arc and beat it down into place as before.

The shed stick is brought down into use again to make the first shed for the third row and the leashes are pulled up, making the second shed for the fourth row. Continue until sufficient heading has been woven.

The arcs are a very important part of weaving technique because the weft must be able to go over and under the warp, which is held at great tension, and yet cover it completely. Beating down in the way demonstrated enables the weaver to achieve complete coverage without the weft being too tight or too loose. If the weft is too tight the selvedge can become pulled in and the finished rug will have an uneven width. It is also likely that the warp will still show and the weft will not lie flat, building up into an uneven line and making it impossible to weave straight across the warp. Alternatively, if the weft is left loose and too long, the rug will have a weak structure.

Once the technique is established, it will continue almost automatically, complete coverage of warp being achieved, but care must be taken in the first few rows. When the heading has been woven to the required depth, cut the weft off at one edge, leaving an end of about 6in.

Fig. 29a, b and c: Beating the weft into position; (d): The weft moving over and under the rigid warp.

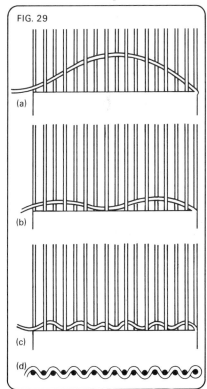

FIG. 29

(a)

(b)

(c)

(d)

Green tapestry *Gwen Mullins*

Yellow Pagoda *Gwen Mullins*

Starting and finishing the weft

When you are a beginner, it is simpler if the weft yarn is thicker than the warp, so that it covers the warp completely. It can be already plied or, if of fine gauge, more than one thickness can be wound on to a shuttle.

To begin weaving, the weft wool must first be fastened into the warp. Here is how it is done: In the diagram (Fig. 30), four threads are being used as one, to make the instructions easier to understand.

If a thick weft wool is being used, unravel the end; if more than one strand of yarn is being used, separate them. Make the first shed with the shed stick. Put the weft through the shed, leaving an end hanging by the selvedge. Divide this and pass half twice around the selvedge and back along the same shed for about $1\frac{1}{2}$in (Fig. 30).

In this way the selvedge has been reinforced and there is only a small place where there is extra weft, which will not show when the following weft picks are in position. Finishing and starting are worked in the same way.

Joining the wefts

In Fig. 30b, four wefts are being used as one, working from right to left. The old weft is divided in half and the ends allowed to hang out of the warp, lying about 2in apart. The new weft, divided in half again, is put into place so that the shorter end overlaps with the longer end of the old weft, and the longer end overlaps the shorter end.

In this way the structure is not weakened, and the two areas where there is extra weft will not show when weaving is continued.

Fig. 30: (a): *Starting and finishing the weft*; (b) *Joining two wefts.*

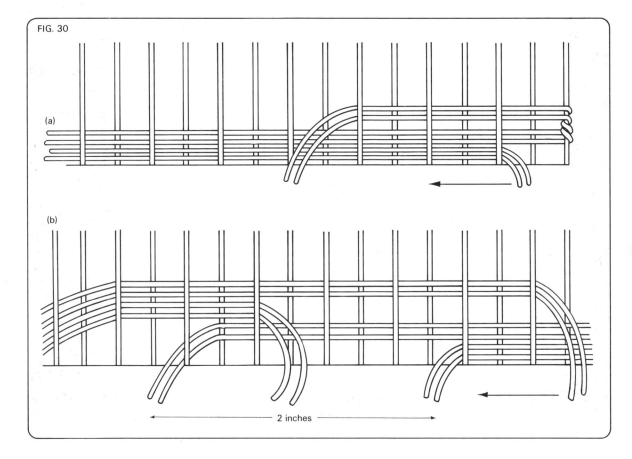

FIG. 30

(a)

(b)

2 inches

The weft ends left hanging are darned down the front of the nearest warp thread for about 1½in and afterwards trimmed. A needle with a large eye and a blunt tip should be used so that the warp is not damaged. It is easier to darn in the ends as you work, while the weaving is still on the loom (Fig. 31).

Make sure that the width of the rug is kept constant throughout weaving and that the heading at both ends is worked to the same depth. When the rug has been woven to the required length, cut it off the loom, allowing enough warp to make the fringe.

Mending a broken warp end

The warp used for rug making is usually very strong and does not break easily, but sometimes it becomes worn and frays, or a knot in the warp might become loosened.

To mend a broken warp end, cut a length of warp thread long enough to reach from the weaving to beyond the leashes or shed stick, plus about 12in.

Knot one end of this thread to the broken thread at the back of the loom and wind the other end round a large pin slipped into the weaving (Fig. 32). Tie the temporary thread firmly in a double bow above the shed sticks, so that the tension of the new thread is the same as the rest of the warp.

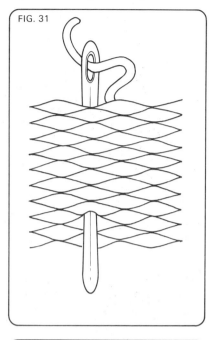

Fig. 31: *Darning in the weft.*

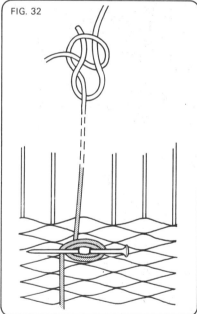

Fig. 32: *Mending a broken warp thread; tie thread round a pin in the weaving and knot other end to the original thread at top of loom, beyond the shed lifting device.*

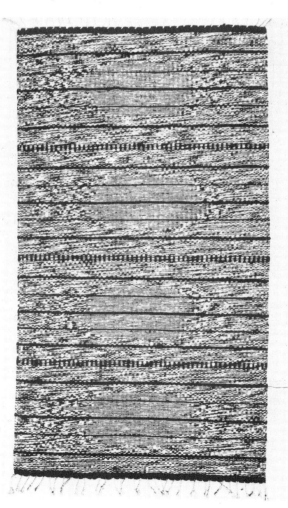

Rug *Peter Collingwood*

Blue Fingers *Gwen Mullins*

Tapestry weaving

In tapestry weaving (for weft-faced rugs) the weft covers the warp completely. The wool is carried from selvedge to selvedge to form a simple area of colour which can be worked to whatever length is required for the design of the rug. When, however, more than one colour is required, two shuttles, each wound with different coloured wool, are used.

Three different effects are possible with two shuttles:
1. Horizontal weft stripes
2. Vertical warp stripes
3. Spots

With the techniques demonstrated in this section, you will begin to see how your own simple rug designs can be worked.

Weft stripes

There are endless permutations of stripes that can be used:
Even stripes – 2/2, (that is, two rows in colour A, two rows in colour B) 4/4, 6/6, or uneven stripes – 2/4, 4/6; 2/2 stripes produce a thin wavy line (Fig. 36).

When weaving stripes up to six threads deep it is not necessary to finish off the wool at the end of each stripe. The wool can be carried up the side of the rug with the selvedge (Fig. 35). This means that the selvedge is thicker in some places than in others but this is not noticeable. If stripes are wider than six threads deep it is better to finish off each stripe individually at the selvedge.

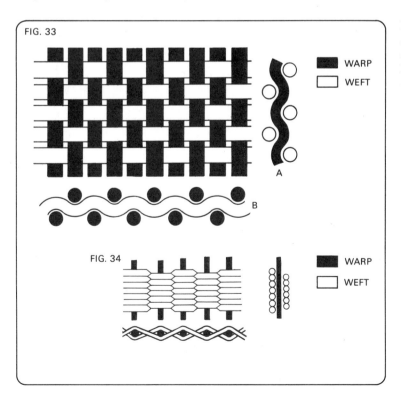

FIG. 33

WARP
WEFT

A

B

FIG. 34

WARP
WEFT

Fig. 33: *The warp and weft crossing, showing the adjustment of both in ordinary weaving.*
Fig. 34: *The weft completely covers the warp in tapestry weaving.*

Detail of tapestry sampler showing bands of graded tone *Gwen Mullins*

If one pick of colour A is woven, and then in the next row a pick of colour B is woven, and so on, these picks will cover the warp in such a way that thin vertical stripes are formed. This method has been used for centuries for vertical stripes and the pattern can be used across the entire width of the rug, or in blocks, to form designs.

Selvedges

When using a thin weft, the threads lie neatly at the selvedge, but when thick rug wool is being used the selvedges can become lumpy and ungainly. This can be overcome by allowing only one of the wefts to wind round the selvedge each time and letting the other miss the selvedge completely. The method is different for even and uneven warps.

If the rug is to be a single unit in itself it is better to have an uneven number of warp threads, so that the colour at the edges is the same. If the rug is to be woven in strips and joined to make a larger rug, an even number of warp threads is required, so that the colour order of the stripes is continuous.

Three rugs *Peter Collingwood*

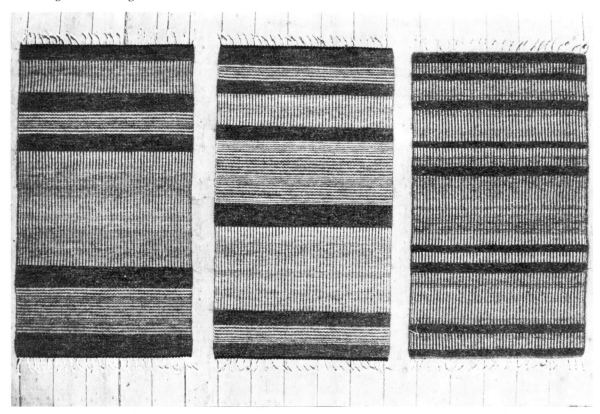

Detail of colour grading in one and one stripes *Lorraine Hughes*

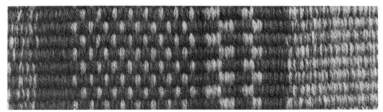

Colour and one and one stripes, detail of sampler *Sarah Surman*

Patterning techniques

Striped and spot patterns

Weaving one and one stripes with an even number of warp threads (Fig. 37).

1. Lift the odd numbered threads and pass A across the warp. It will miss the right selvedge.
2. Lift the even numbered threads. Wrap B twice *downwards* round the right selvedge and then pass it from right to left.
3. Lift the odd numbered threads. Wrap A twice *upwards* round the left selvedge and pass from left to right.
4. Lift the even numbered threads, pass B from left to right. You will see that B misses the left selvedge. Repeat this process.

Weaving one and one stripes with an uneven number of warp threads (Fig. 38). Start with A and B at the right, with B lying over the selvedge thread.

1. Lift the odd numbered threads and pass A from right to left. This thread misses the selvedge completely and moves vertically upwards from its previous row, making a small loop at the back of the rug.
2. Lift the even numbered threads, wrap B twice downwards round the selvedge and pass from right to left.
3. Lift the odd numbered threads and pass A from left to right. It leaves a loop on the back of the rug as before, but on the left.
4. Lift the even numbered threads, wrap B twice downwards round the selvedge and pass from left to right. Repeat.

Reversing the colour in one and one stripes (Fig. 39). Colour A lies over even numbered threads and is going to change and lie over the odd numbered threads.

1. Weave two rows of colour A.
2. Twist B twice downwards round the right selvedge and pass from right to left. This will make a float over two threads at the right selvedge.
3. Take A over this float, under the right selvedge and pass it from right to left.
4. Weave B from left to right, missing the left selvedge.
5. Twist A twice downwards round the left selvedge then pass from left to right. Continue in the same manner.

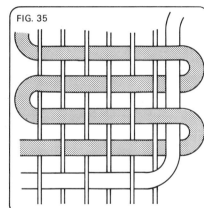

Fig. 35 : *Carrying the weft up the selvedge.*

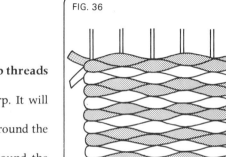

Fig. 36 : *Two and two stripes produce a thin wavy line.*

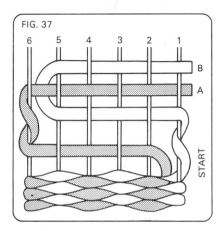

Fig. 37 : *One and one stripes with even number of warp threads, showing the four weft picks in position but not beaten into place.*

Spots. Spots are produced by weaving one pick of one colour and two, three, four or more picks of a second colour and then repeating the sequence.

If there is an odd number of picks between the single rows the spots will lie vertically, and if there is an even number of picks the spots will lie in a half drop position. The diagrams show spots woven on an odd numbered warp so that they lie within the boundaries of the rug. If strips of weaving are to be joined, they should be woven on an even numbered warp.

Weaving spots with an odd number of picks between them (Fig. 40). A is the colour making the spots, and B the colour that is weaving to the selvedges. Start with A on the right and B on the left.

1. Weave three of B, twisting it twice downwards on the last pick.
2. Weave one of A from right to left, missing the selvedge thread.
3. Weave three of B, ending in the same manner as before.
4. Weave A from left to right, missing the selvedge thread. Repeat this process.

Weaving spots with an even number of picks between them (Fig. 41).

1. Weave two picks of B (background colour), from left to right and back.
2. Weave one pick of A from right to left.
3. Weave two picks of B. It will miss the left selvedge.
4. Twist A twice downwards and pass from left to right.
5. Pass B over the float made by A at the beginning of the last row, and under the selvedge. Repeat the sequence.

Meet and separate weave (Fig. 42). This is a variation of a tapestry

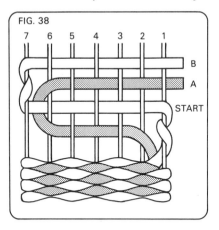

Fig. 38: *One and one stripes with an uneven number of threads in the warp.*

Fig. 39: *Reversing the colours in one and one stripes.*

Fig. 40: *Spots with an odd number of picks between them.*

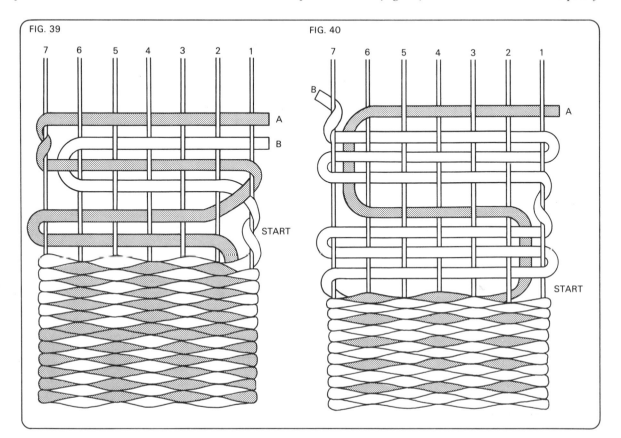

technique. In tapestry it is used to shade from one area to another, so giving an area of mixed colour. The result will be three areas of colour, A, B and a mixture of A and B.

Method of working
Lift the even-numbered ends. Insert colour B from the left and colour A from the right, and bring them out between the raised ends 8 and 10.

2. Lift the odd-numbered ends and insert A and B back to their own selvedge, between the raised ends 9 and 11.

3. Lift the even-numbered ends and insert A and B into this shed, bringing them out between 4 and 6.

4. Lift the odd-numbered ends and insert A and B back to their own selvedge, between 5 and 7.

As seen in the diagram, this produces an area of white on the left, mixed white and black in the middle and black on the right.

By using this technique, patterns of varying complexity can be made, by altering the points at which the wefts meet and separate.

You can also use three colours which, with the two meeting areas, will produce five colours when woven. The system of weaving is the same as with two colours, but it means that the centre colour never touches the selvedge. It is best to move the centre colour first to establish the meeting points between the colours. This type of design is planned on squared paper, each square marking the point where the weft crosses the warp (Figs. 43: (a)).

Block patterns
Kilim or inlay rugs When patterns are introduced into tapestry woven rugs, they are known as Kilim or inlay rugs. Kilim is the word used for a slit tapestry woven rug. The world kilim (also spelt kelim, khelim, ghilleem) is supposedly related to the Arabic word for curtain, suggesting that their early use was as a decorative hanging textile. Kilims were also used as blankets, horse trappings, bed covers, saddle-bags and as a strong material for wrapping around goods, so necessary in nomadic life.

Columns *Gwen Mullins*

Fig. 41: *Spots with an even number of picks between them.*

Fig. 42: *Meet and separate weave, using two wefts.*

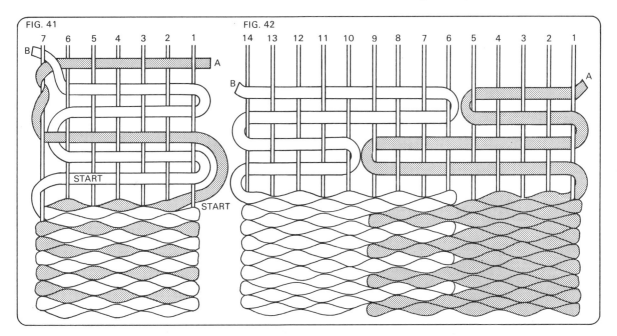

Fig. 44: *The slit formed by the adjacent non-linking blocks of colour. If this becomes too big it will make a weakness in the structure.*

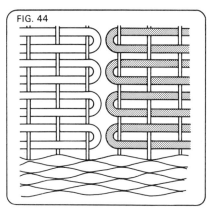

Fig. 43: (a): *Meet and separate weave. Plan for making a diamond and result* (b).

The earliest known kilim was found in a site near Troy and was dated as being made before 2500 BC. It was made in yellow, red, blue and black and was made up of the simple geometric motifs found in kilims today. The typical feature of the kilim – the slit between adjacent colour areas – makes them rather unsuitable for Western floor coverings, although the more sturdy varieties can take a great deal of hard wear.

In kilim rugs, the design is built up of small areas of solid colour, each woven with an individual weft and not interlocking with adjacent weft areas. A vertical slit is thus formed between areas which may be up to $\frac{3}{4}$in long. The characteristic diamond, triangle and lozenge shapes in kilim designs occur because the coloured areas are arranged so that the edges of the patterns are stepped in order to prevent the slits being too long (Fig. 44).

The number of weft picks needed in each step of the join depend on the thickness of the weft yarn. In the diagram, the steps are shown as either single or double weft picks. In practice the number would be greater than this and can only be judged in relationship to the number of warp ends per inch, the thickness of the weft yarn and the type of shape to be made. For example, in Fig. 45, the diagonal is 45 deg to the horizontal. Using thick yarn, only a few picks would be needed in each step, but with thinner yarn double or treble the number of picks is needed in each step.

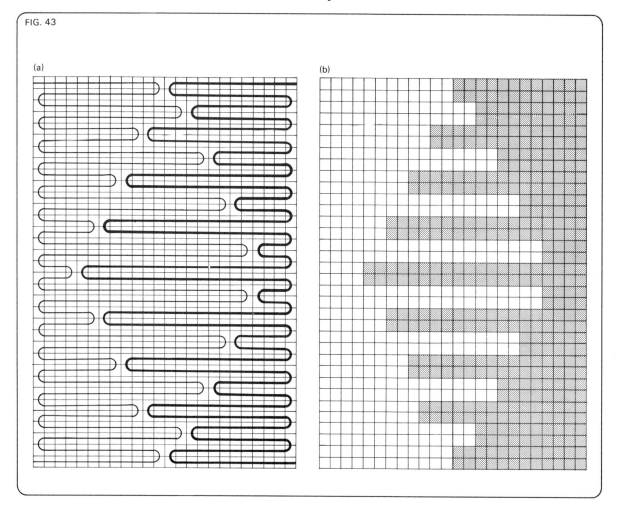

FIG. 43

(a)

(b)

The weft picks can be used in two ways, either in parallel motion, which means that they are all started from the same side, or in contrary motion, the weft picks in adjacent blocks running in the opposite direction (Fig. 46).

The second method is suitable when very simple shapes are used, that do not divide around another central shape. When this happens it is likely that somewhere in the design the picks are going to be forced to run in parallel, so it would have been better to have them running in parallel from the beginning. Most kilim rugs are woven in parallel movement.

Linking the blocks The blocks are joined by linking first one weft pick round the warp thread that is common to adjacent blocks, and on the next row linking the weft pick from the other block around the same warp thread, so that on one row the weft pick will link round the warp thread, and on the next it will miss it, and so on.

Each block of colour has its individual shuttle of yarn. A small bobbin or finger hank is easiest to manage. Variations can be made in the depth of the common linking area of the colours. For example, the wefts can flow into each other at their edges (Fig. 47) by forming a zig-zag pattern, linking over one, then two, then three common warp threads, and back again. Remember there would be more than two threads per link, depending on the thickness of the yarn.

Fig. 45: *Kilim: a diagonal block of colour should be at 45 deg with the horizontal.*
Fig. 46: *Kilim: joining blocks of colour, the wefts moving in contrary motion.*

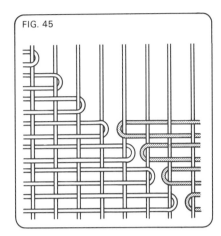

FIG. 45

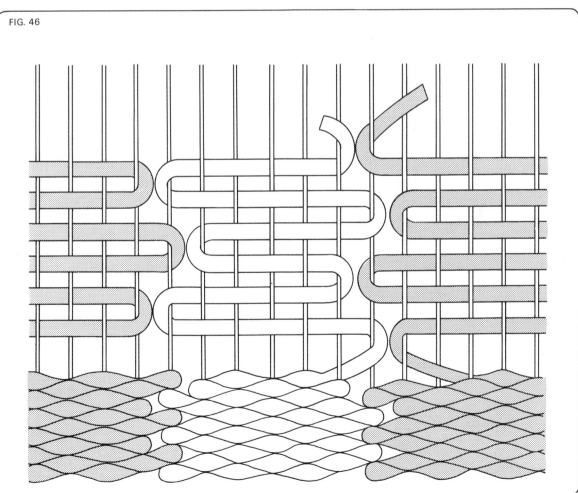

FIG. 46

Kilim sampler *Gwen Mullins*

Detail of kilim sampler *Gwen Mullins*

An alternative variation is achieved by forming a brick junction by linking over three threads, back to the border while the other colour links over the three threads and so on.

Designing kilim   The kilim design is drafted on squared paper, each square equalling one warp thread. Do a test strip of weaving with the weft to see how many weft threads there are per vertical inch. This is necessary because otherwise you may end up with a rather flattened version of your design. You can then weave following your square paper plan. When you are more experienced, the design can be drawn directly on to the warp, but this method is not advised at the beginning.

Shapes can be woven in total and then the background woven around them, but one rule must always be followed. You must never enclose the acute angle, ie, the angle between the horizontal and the weaving. If you do this you will be unable to weave in this area because you cannot get a shed (Fig. 48).

Soumak   The decorative technique of soumak stitch can be traced back to 2000 BC, the date of some linen fragments found in Switzerland. Later examples of the technique have been found in Egypt, Peru and Persia and it has also been used by many primitive people, including the inhabitants of New Caledonia and Guiana.

In appearance, soumak is decorative, forming a ridge raised above the level of the plain weave. It is worked on the flat warp, ie, when there is no shed open.

Fig. 47: *Kilim: vertical colour junctions; (a) zig-zag junction, (b) brick junction.*

Fig. 48: *Weaving a complete block. (a) is incorrect, because it is impossible to make a shed in the two bottom triangles. (b) Can be woven by first weaving the background and then weaving the triangle in the middle.*

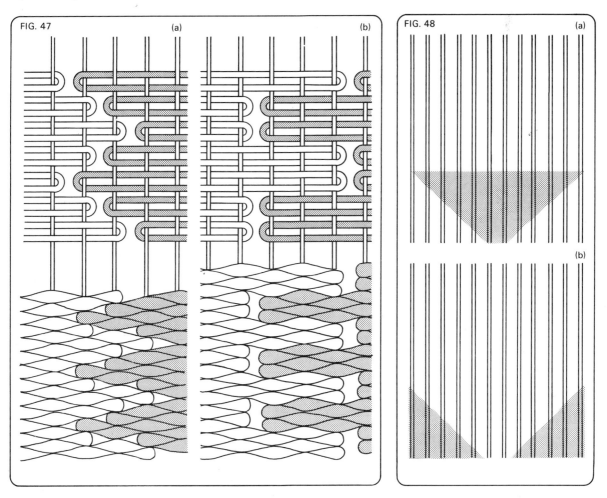

41

Detail of kilim showing weft face techniques *Hamlyn Picture Library*

Soumak – raised motif

In soumak, there are basically two wefts. One is the ground weft that weaves with the warp to make a normal tapestry structure and the other is the soumak weft, which crosses the warp at intervals, wrapping round the warp more in the manner of embroidery than weaving.

The simplest form is 2/1 soumak. This means the weft is carried over two warp threads and under one – but there are other variations over which it can be worked – 4/2, in which the weft goes over four and under two, 3/2, 6/3 and 9/3. The closest texture is given by 2/1 soumak and this is most used in rugs. The other variations give very much longer floats (the threads which are not woven or caught into the structure), and would be impractical for floor rugs.

Method of working soumak (Fig. 49).
1. Make two rows of plain weave.
2. Pass the soumak weft over two warp threads and back under one, coming out between the weft and the plain weave.
3. Continue in this manner across the warp. This will make a band of raised weft that slants from bottom right to left (Fig. 49).
4. Make two rows of plain weave.

When weaving back from the other direction, pass the weft in the same manner, coming out between the soumak and the plain weave. This makes a band slanting from bottom left to top right.

The two rows seen together make a series of 'v' shapes pointing to the left. By working in the opposite direction, the reverse shapes are made. Soumak can be worked in bands across the whole width of the rug or can be used to make blocks.

Starting and finishing the ends of the soumak weft is achieved by weaving the end of the thread into the same shed as the next plain weave weft, for a short distance. The soumak should not be woven to the selvedge; instead, work in the same way as for the selvedge when making tufts (page 44).

Pulling out loops

This is a very good way of adding texture to a rug. The length of the loop can be adjusted to the needs of the design, and if it is long enough it can be cut to make a kind of tuft.

Method of working. With a contrast-coloured cotton thread, mark on the warp threads where a loop is required. Weave in the usual way as far as the mark and beat the weft into place. Make a weft loop of the required size at the marked point and pull it into place. Continue to weave the weft in the normal way (Fig. 50).

Loops can have rows of plain weave in between, or can be made in alternate rows of weaving. They can be massed to form textured areas in the design or scattered to form background interest.

Knotting or tufting

Rya is a Scandinavian term applied to long tufted rugs. Originally, rya rugs were used in Scandinavian countries as bedcovers, as well as floor coverings and wall hangings. Today rya is used mainly as a floor covering and wall hanging.

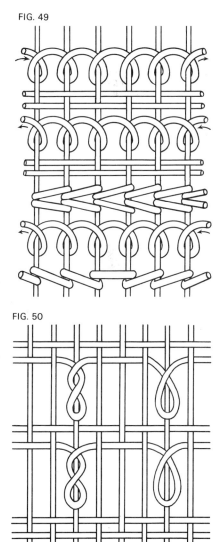

Fig. 49: *Soumak, showing the method of working and the finished result.*
Fig. 50: *Pulling the loops.*

FIG. 49

FIG. 50

Fig. 51: *Length of tufts. The more tapestry weave between the tufts the longer the tufts should be, so that two-thirds of the previous row tufts are covered.*

Fig. 52: *Weaving the selvedge.*

The colours in a rya can be mixed very freely and give an appearance of great richness and depth. Because it is three-dimensional, the light falls at a different angle on each single thread, changing the colour from light to dark. The length of the pile, the material of the pile yarn, the amount of plain weave and the spacing of the knots are some of the elements that can be varied endlessly to produce rugs of different thickness, resilience, texture and weight.

Weaving rya

The knots are tied into the warp by hand and have two or more rows of plain tapestry weave between each row of knots. If there is only a narrow strip of weaving between the rows of knots, they will stand on end and the deeper the space between the rows of tufting the flatter the tufts will lie. The knots are not taken to each selvedge because this would cause the rug to curl at the edges. The selvedge is woven with a strong weft to make a protective edging to the rug (Fig. 51).

The weft is woven in plain weave until the point where a row of tufts is required. The tufts are knotted into position over two ends right across the warp when the warp is closed, ie, there is no shed. They must not be pulled too tight because this will affect the spacing of the warp and cause difficulty in weaving the following rows of plain weaving. Two or more threads (an even number) are left for the selvedge. The selvedge, or border, is then woven to the correct height on these threads, so that the new row of plain tapestry weave goes right across the warp from selvedge to selvedge and the same number of weft picks are woven on the selvedge or border threads and pushed firmly into place (Fig. 52).

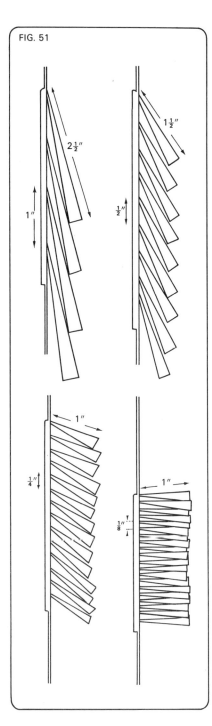

FIG. 51

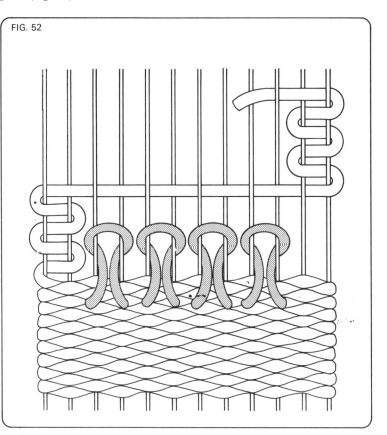

FIG. 52

44

Care must be taken over the size of yarn used for tufts, because, if it is not thick enough, gaps will show between each knot and if too thick, the finished rug will buckle. The thickness of the weft varies according to the spacing of the warp. Thicker weft is used if there are only a few threads to the inch in the warp and thinner weft is used if there are more threads to the inch in the warp. For example: if there are four ends per inch in the warp, use two or three threads of two-ply carpet wool in the weft; if there are six ends per inch, use two threads, and if there are eight ends per inch, use one thread of two-ply carpet wool.

Turkish or Ghiordes knot

There are three ways of working this knot:

1. Knotting from continuous yarn and cutting each knot as it is tied (Fig. 53).

a. Prepare the yarn for the tufts by winding it into a ball.

b. Leave the first two or four ends (or more for a border) and start with the first warp end after this on the left-hand side of the rug.

c. Take the yarn under the first warp end, starting from the right side of the thread, then over the first and second and back between the two ends and below the knot.

d. Pull down the knot regulating the length of the tuft.

e. Cut it to the required length.

Continue to make the knots in this way either from one side to the other, or according to the design.

2. Knotting with cut lengths of pile yarn (Figs. 54, 55, 56). This is a slower technique, but this method lends itself to many rich colour changes.

a. Wind the yarn round a long square section stick with a groove in one of its long sides.

b. Cut along the groove.

You will now have a number of pieces of yarn of equal length. All the colours needed can be cut in this way and sorted into containers.

c. Place the yarn over two warp ends and bring the ends under the warp threads and out through the space between them.

d. Pull the knot into position.

Continue knotting in this way across the warp.

3. Knotting over a guide rod (Fig. 57). This method is useful if a uniform length of tufts has to be maintained and if a colour change does

Fig. 53: *Turkish knot, method 1. Knotting with continuous yarn and cutting each knot as it is tied.*
Fig. 54: *Method 2. Knotting with cut lengths of pile yarn.*
Fig. 55: *The grooved stick over which yarn is wound for method 2.*
Fig. 56: *Knotting in different directions to alter direction of pile.*
Fig. 57: *Turkish knot, method 3. Knotting over a guide rod.*

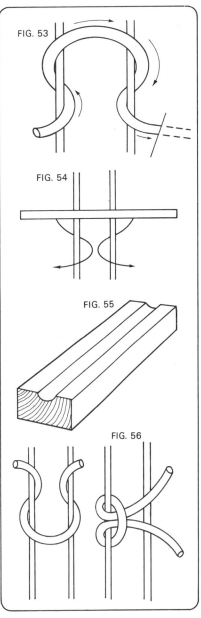

FIG. 53

FIG. 54

FIG. 55

FIG. 56

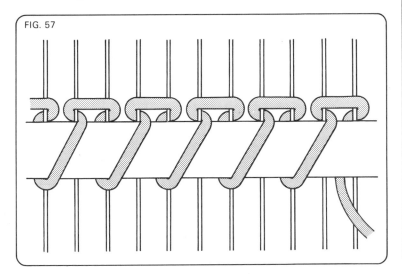

FIG. 57

not occur too often. The length of the tufts depends on the width of the stick. Therefore, for different lengths of tufts, different widths of stick must be used.

a. Wind the yarn on to a small shuttle.

b. Take the yarn under one warp thread from the right and over two towards the right, back under one so that it comes out between the two warp threads.

c. Put the stick in place and take the yarn round the stick and start making the knot again. Continue in this manner for the required number of tufts.

d. When the whole row of tufts is completed, cut the loops.

Preventing the knots showing at the end of the rug If all the tufts are put in the weaving so that the ends of the tufts lie towards the weaver, when the rug is finished the knots will show (Fig. 58). To prevent this happening, gradually alter the direction in which the tufts lie over the last four rows of tufts.

a. Start with the fourth row from the end and reverse every fourth knot.

b. In the third row reverse every third knot.

c. In the second row reverse every second knot.

d. In the last row reverse every knot.

The tufts will now lie in the opposite direction and so cover the knots (Fig. 58).

Fig. 58: *Preventing knots showing at end of rug by changing direction of knots.*

FIG. 58

Finishing the ends of the rug

You have now finished weaving your rug and cut it from the loom, leaving the long warp ends. The ends of a rug can be finished off in three ways:

1. With a series of tassels
2. With a deep fringe
3. With a smooth edge

The choice of method depends on the type of design and where the rug is going to be used. As a general rule, if the rug has a complicated design, keep the fringe simple; if the rug itself is simple, a feature can be made of the fringe. The fringe should not be too thin. Try different scales until the correct density is found.

Tassels
The simple knot
1. Decide how many threads are to form the knot – an even number.
2. Divide the group of threads in half.
3. Hold the left-hand group taut and pass the right-hand group over and back under the left-hand group and the right.
4. Pass the right-hand group down through itself; a knot is made by the right group over the left, which is hanging free.
5. Hold the left threads firmly and push the right group tightly against the end of the weaving. This will make a tassel which lies flatly at the end of the rug. This knot can also be used in combination with other knots to make a neat edge (Fig. 60).

Plaiting
Everyone knows how to plait or braid, and the technique needs no elaboration. The size and complication of the plait depends on the individual. Finish the plait by making an overhand knot. Pull this tight by pulling the individual threads into place (Fig. 59).

FIG. 59

Fig. 59 : *Plaiting fringes.*
Fig. 60 : *Stages of the simple knot.*
Hold thread over which knot is being made firmly, so knot may be pushed easily into place against weaving.

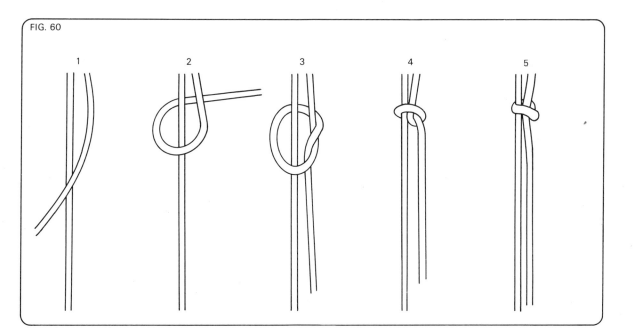

FIG. 60

   1   2   3   4   5

Double half-hitch

1. Divide the group of threads in half. This makes a knobblier tassel.
2. Pass the right thread over and then under the left, coming out between the right and the left. Pull tight.
3. Pass the left over and then under the right, coming out between the right and the left. Pull tight.
4. Continue in this way until the required length is reached.
5. Make an overhand knot, pulling the threads tight individually (Figs. 61, 62).

FIG. 61

1 2 3

Fig. 61: *Stages of making double half hitches. Knot B over A and then A over B. Repeat. Make an overhand knot to finish, then trim.*
Fig. 62: *Fringe in double half hitches.*

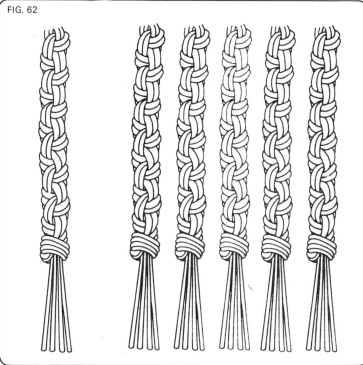

FIG. 62

Multi coloured beige *Roger Oates*

A corded fringe

The diagram (Fig. 63) shows the working of this in singles but it can be made in doubles, trebles etc (Fig. 64).

1. Hold A and B diagonally from left to right. Cross C over both A and B and D under B and over A. Pass C back down between A and B and out between A and D.

2. Cross B over A and C and out between C and A.

3. Cross D over C and B and back under B. Continue in this manner until the cord is the required length.

4. Make an overhand knot to hold the cord in position.

Fig. 63: (a): *Cross C and D and A and back under A;* (b): *Cross B over A and C and back under C;* (c): *Cross D over C and B and back under B;* (d, e): *continue;* (f): *Tie an overhand knot firmly to hold cord in position.*
Fig. 64: *A corded fringe.*

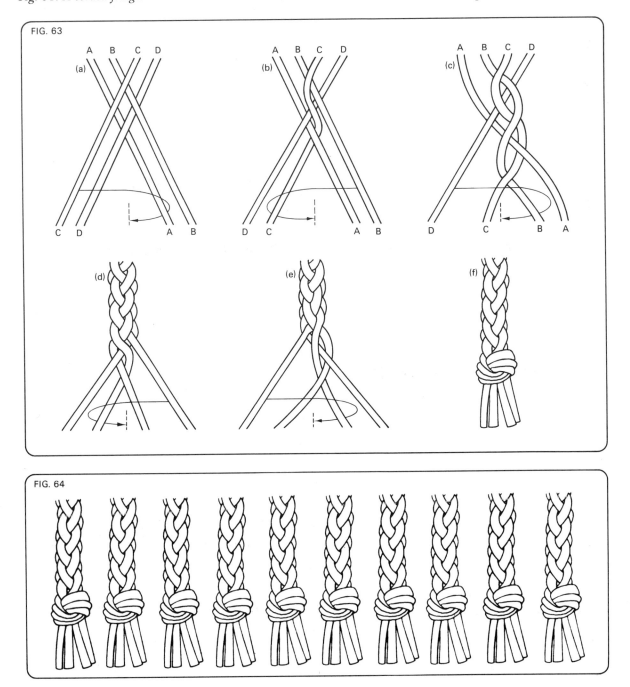

Deep fringes
Overhand knot
Divide the ends of the warp into groups of the size required.
1. Make a row of overhand knots as close to the last row of weaving as possible.
2. Divide these groups of threads into half and, using half from one group and half of the adjacent group, make a row of overhand knots so that they lie between the knots in the row above.
3. Repeat this process until the fringe is the required length.
4. Trim the last row of knots (Fig. 65).

Twisted fringe with overhand knots (Fig. 66).
Divide the ends of the warp into groups of the size required.
1. Make a row of overhand knots as close to the last row of weaving as possible.
2. Take the right half of the threads from the first group on the left and the left half of the threads from the next group. Holding them parallel, tie an overhand knot at the required length of the fringe.
3. Twist this group so that the left-hand threads lie on the left again, and the right on the right. A twist will then be made at the top near the row of overhand knots.
4. Take the right-hand group of the second knot and pass this from underneath through the loop between the twist and the bottom overhand knot.
5. Take the left group of the third knot and pass this from underneath through the loop made by the previous group at the top next to the twist.

Fig. 65: *Overhand knot. Make a row of overhand knots, then divide threads and knot half the threads from two adjacent knots together.*

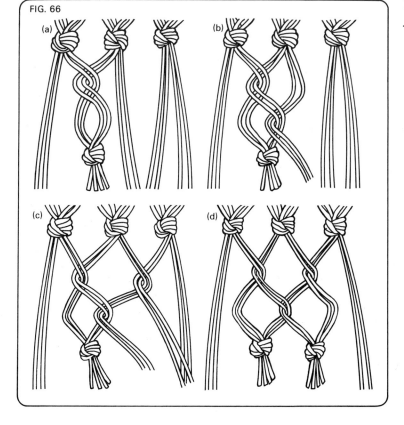

Fig. 66: *Stages of working a twisted fringe with overhand knots.*

Anger *Gwen Mullins*

Rug, woven in two strips and joined *Mary Bennett*

6. Holding the last working groups together, make an overhand knot level with the knot at the bottom of the fringe.

In this manner the twist and lower knot lie between the row of knots at the top, just below the weaving and two rows of linking threads are made. If you require the fringe to be longer, more twists would have to be made in the first working group and the procedure adjusted.

The work continues across the fringe by looping first with the right half of the left group and then with the left half of the right group. There will be a group left hanging at the left and right ends of the completed fringe. Loop these downwards through the adjacent bottom loop, untie the knot holding these groups and retie, including the extra threads (Fig. 67).

Fig. 67: *Twisted fringe with overhand knots.*

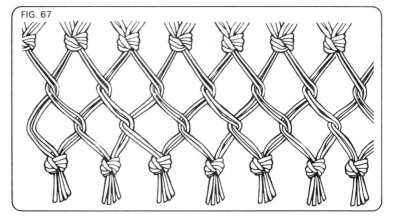

FIG. 67

Interwoven fringe with overhand knots

Divide the ends of the warp into groups of the size required and make a row of overhand knots as close to the last row of weaving as possible.

1. Divide each knotted group of threads in half.
2. Arrange these groups so that they lie at an angle of 45 deg with the end of the weaving and are interwoven (Fig. 68). The threads lying from left to right become the warp; the threads lying from right to left become the weft.
3. Continue weaving on these until the required depth is reached.
4. Knot the ends of the fringe with overhand knots. The threads at the edge turn and become warp if they were weft and vice versa. The weaving need not end in a straight line, but can be shaped at the edge and knotted accordingly (Fig. 68).

Fig. 68: *Interwoven fringe with overhand knots.*

FIG. 68

Flat knot fringe with overhand knots (Fig. 69).

The flat knot is a reef knot that lies over a centre core. It is made by crossing the left thread A over the centre core. This means that, if worked normally, A will always lie on the front. B is then taken over A and under both A and the centre core and brought out between A and the centre, on the other side.

The first part of the reef knot has been made over the centre threads. B lies on the left and A on the right. Cross A back over the top of the centre threads and take B over the top of A and back under the centre to its own side. Pull tightly into place. If these are repeated in verticals they make another variation of the tassel.

To make the fringe, group the threads and make a row of flat knots as close to the weaving as possible. For the next row, make the flat knot with the centre threads, using the other threads as the core. Continue in this manner, making alternate rows of knots, until the required length is reached. Finish the ends with a row of overhand knots. The fringe can be varied by having more than one knot in a row. They can be any length and will make oval instead of diamond shapes between the knots (Fig. 70).

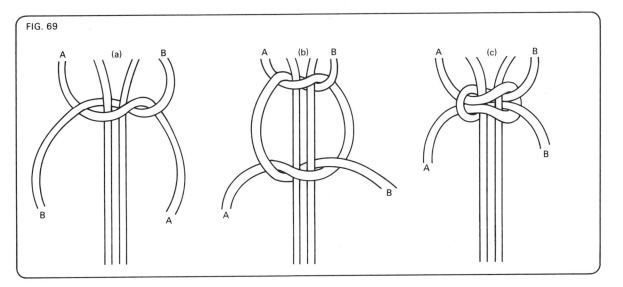

FIG. 69

FIG. 70

Fig. 69: *Three stages of making a flat knot.*

Fig. 70: *Flat knot fringe with overhand knots.*

Hanging Rug *Tony Pugh*

Lichen South Downs *Gwen Mullins*

Woven edge

In this edge the warp threads are going to become the weft and will weave with each other across the width of the rug. Start at the left and weave the first warp thread, A, along the warp for about 2in, bringing it out on the surface at this point and pulling it firmly into position. Then weave B along the warp in the opposite shed, bringing it out on the surface next to A. Weave C in the next shed, bringing it out next to B. Continue in this way across the warp until you reach the right selvedge. There will be a group of warp threads left. These can be knotted, plaited or corded and finished with an overhand knot and clipped (Fig. 71).

This technique makes a smooth edge if care is taken in pulling the threads firmly into place. The ends left on the surface of the rug can either be cut close to the surface, or darned up into the warp and cut off.

Figs. 71: (a), (b): *Woven edge. Weave A for about 2in, then B for 2in, etc, across the warp; Knot or cord the remaining threads, finishing with an overhand knot.*

Fig. 72: *Joining two strips of rug.*

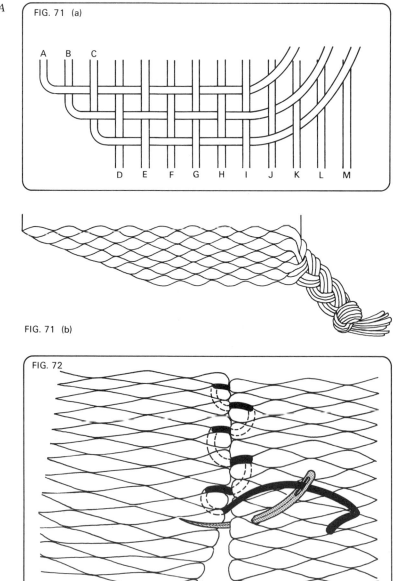

FIG. 71 (a)

A B C

D E F G H I J K L M

FIG. 71 (b)

FIG. 72

Weaving a large rug in strips

If you want to make a rug bigger than you are able to weave on your loom, it must be woven in strips and then joined. Make a full-size plan of the complete rug. Decide where the strips are going to join. Weave the first strip of the rug, writing the number of weft picks used in each section of the pattern on your plan. This is necessary in order to make sure that the pattern will match as accurately as possible when weaving the next strip. Weave all the strips required for the rug.

Joining the strips
1. Fringe all the strips at one end.
2. Sew the strips together, starting at the fringed end and stopping short of the unfringed ends.
3. Draw out a plan of the rug on the floor with chalk, marking out the exact edges in the most suitable way.
4. Put the rug on the plan with the fringe on one end line and the sides on the side lines. The fourth line shows where the other fringe should be.
5. Unweave the end of the rug to bring the fringe to the right place. If the main picks of the rug are not even, adjust the length by unpicking the correct amount of the main picks and then slide the string picks down the warp into position.
6. Sew up to the corrected ends of the strips and fringe across the rug.

This procedure is necessary in order to get a rectangular rug and not a parallelogram. Before sewing, secure the strips about every 2ft with a temporary tie to prevent them moving (Fig. 72). Sew the strips together with a curved needle, using warp yarn that has been dyed to a suitable matching colour. Insert the needle into the first warp interspace of one strip, out between the two strips and then into the first warp interspace of the other strip, out between the two strips and so on.

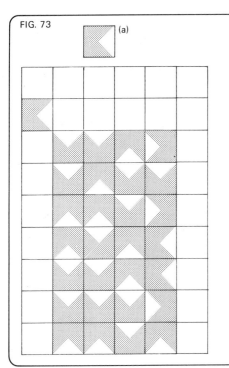

FIG. 73

(a)

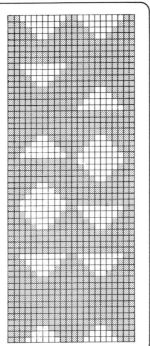

Fig. 73: (a): *Geometric unit used in random repeat to produce idea for a rug design;* (b and c): *Sections of rug design put on to squared paper.*

Kazak rug, Caucasian, 19th century. The bold geometric motifs and large
areas of white are characteristic of Kazak pieces *Hamlyn Picture Library*

Red, green, yellow, purple and blue *Roger Oates*

Designing for a rug

Finding inspiration

You have decided that you want to make a woven rug. You have also decided where you wish to use your rug, either as a floor covering or a wall hanging. The situation will determine the size of the rug and how strong it will have to be. You have established the limitations in which you must work. Now you will decide what kind of pattern or surface texture the rug is to have.

The inspiration or source of idea for a design can be found in a number of different places. Everyone has different ways of looking at the world around them and they are influenced by their environment, as well as their personal likes and dislikes. Some people only like things that are orderly and structured, others seem to prefer the atmospheric and abstract.

Ideas for shapes, pattern and colour are all around us. Natural forms – flowers, trees, leaves, bark, rocks, shells, crystals, bones, birds, fish etc – can provide a limitless source for ideas. Man-made objects are another source; buildings, scaffolding, chimneys, magazine photographs, lettering, newsprint, household objects and so on.

Fig. 74: (a): *Symmetrical pattern;*
(b): *Asymmetrical pattern.*
Fig. 75: (a): *Spot pattern;*
(b): *Counter-change.*

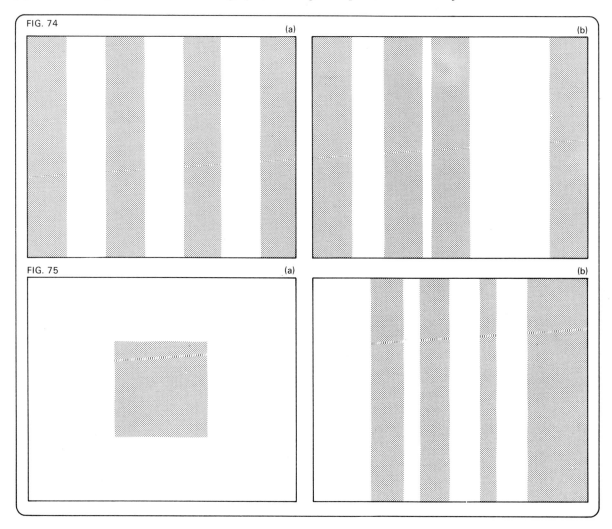

FIG. 74 (a) (b)

FIG. 75 (a) (b)

Patterns within a rectangle

A rug is often rectangular in shape and simple effective patterns can be made within this shape. The structure of weaving itself is based on threads interlacing at right angles, and so patterns based on geometric shapes are most suitable when designing. It can be:

1. Symmetrical or even in balance.

2. Assymmetrical, which means that the focal point in the design is not central.

3. A shape that is free within the rectangle, such as a spot pattern.

4. In counterchange, where the pattern repeats itself so that one unit is, for instance, dark and the other light.

5. In repeating pattern.

6. In gradation so that it moves from a small to a large pattern in easy stages.

7. In half reverse (mirror image).

8. In quarter reverse, which means that each quarter is in mirror image to its neighbours.

See Figs. 73 to 77, for examples of these designs.

These are basic pattern forms that can be applied to the design of rugs; they may be as simple or as complicated as one wishes within this framework.

Fig. 76: (a): *Repeating pattern.*
(b): *Gradation in the size of stripes in mirror image.*
Fig. 77: (a): *Half-reverse pattern, or mirror image;* (b): *Quarter-reverse pattern.*

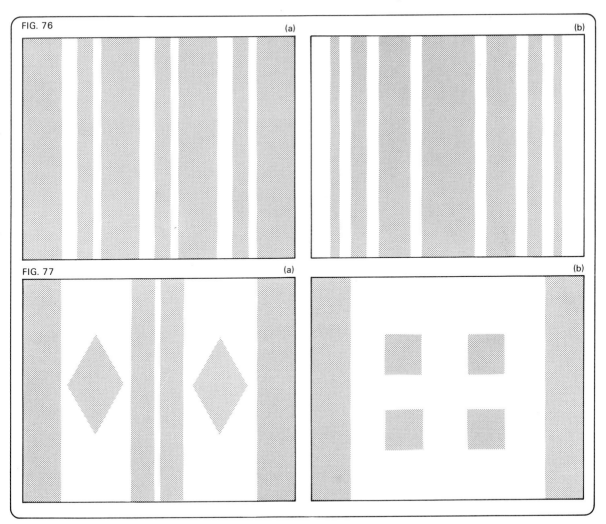

FIG. 76   (a)   (b)

FIG. 77   (a)   (b)

Pattern making using small geometric shapes should always be kept as simple as possible. The way in which the rug is woven will add interest and emphasis to the design and an over-complicated pattern will only disturb and detract from the quality of the weave.

Ways with triangles

In Figs. 80 and 81, a triangle has been arranged to form bands of triangles, zig-zags and a combination of large and small triangles. The pattern is altered further by some of the triangles being dark and some light, and by emphasising some parts by introducing a third colour.

A pattern can also be made by stating the background rather than the shape itself. This is seen in the zig-zags made by the triangles and in the detail of the sampler.

The possibilities in design using just one shape is so great that it is well worth concentrating on a particular theme and exploring all the ways that this can be used, rather than moving too rapidly from one pattern to another. See Figs. 82, 83 and 84.

Fig. 81 : *Triangles in three tones on squared paper.*

FIG. 81

66

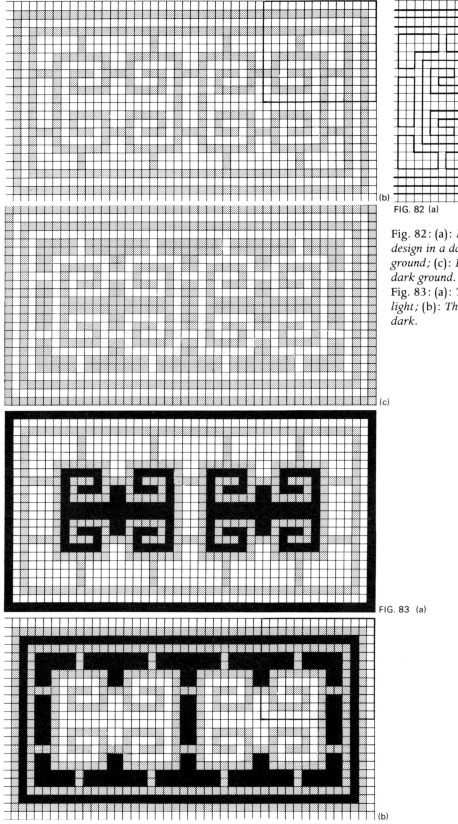

(b)

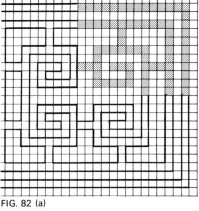

FIG. 82 (a)

(c)

Fig. 82: (a): *Pattern unit;* (b): *Unit in design in a dark colour on a light ground;* (c): *In a light colour on a dark ground.*

Fig. 83: (a): *Three tones with dark on light;* (b): *Three tones with light on dark.*

FIG. 83 (a)

(b)

Fig. 84: (a): *Three tones making a dark band on a light background;* (b): *Three tones making a light band on a dark background.*

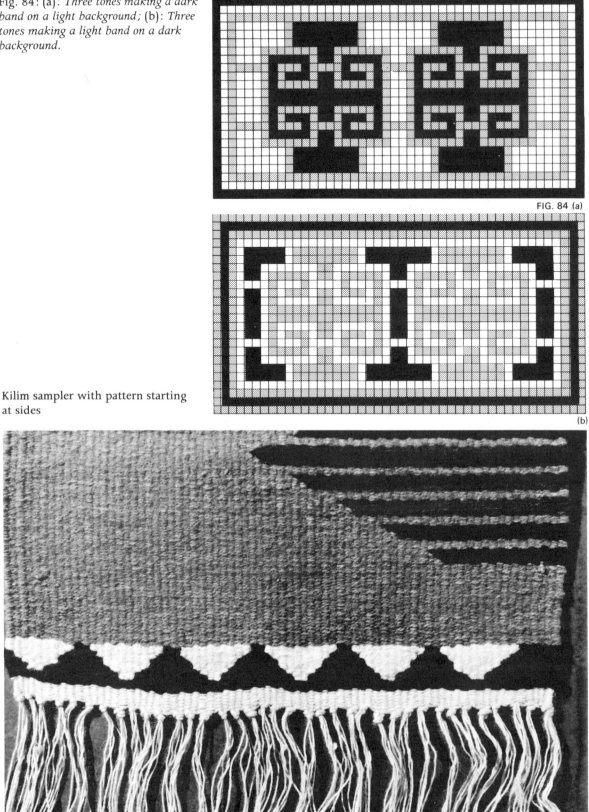

FIG. 84 (a)

(b)

Kilim sampler with pattern starting at sides

Suitability of purpose

When anything is designed, the first requirement is that the object fulfils its function and is suitable for its purpose. If it fails to do this, however beautiful or desirable it may be in other ways, the design is bad because it cannot do what it was meant to do. A teapot that cannot pour is no use to anyone, a container that will not hold the required amount a failure. So, when one is thinking about rug design, one must bear in mind that a rug can be used in three ways; as a floor covering, a bed cover or as a wall hanging. A bedroom rug does not have to be as hardwearing as one used in a sitting room and a hall rug would have to be much tougher than both.

As a floor covering
A floor rug must be of the correct size for its situation; if it is too big it will not fit in and if it is too small it will look extremely odd. It must be capable of standing an amount of wear and tear. This varies according to the type of room, of course.

The colour is very important; this will either make the rug a focal point, or enable it to blend in with the rest of the furniture or fittings.

The design of the rug – its pattern or lack of pattern – is another important factor; this will be affected by, and affect, the general appearance of its surroundings.

As a bed cover
A rug that is to be used as a covering has to be light enough to be lifted easily and, once on the bed, if it is intended to be used as a blanket, it must not be too weighty for comfort. It must, of course, be the right size for the bed and this means including the fall on three sides in the overall measurements.

A most attractive bed cover can be made from a woven rug by working a piece to the length and width of the bed and then mounting the weaving on to a larger, fabric bed cover.

As a wall hanging
A woven wall hanging is usually one of two types; either it is a floor rug of such fine quality and technique that it would be better preserved by hanging it, or it is a specially designed rug, meant to be seen on a vertical surface.

If it is to be the latter, the design is approached in a different way from the previous types of rug mentioned. The rug will be looked at from one direction only – vertically, instead of being seen from all sides and the colour and design will become a focal point on the wall of a room.

Wall rugs can provide tremendous design scope for weavers because all kinds of weft materials and techniques can be used that would not be suitable in a harder wearing floor rug.

One last point to remember; the size of the shapes in relationship to the area of the rug is most important. They must be large enough to be seen clearly at a distance as well as being interesting to look at when close at hand. The weave itself, seen when working on the loom, at close quarters, has a totally different appearance and importance and if it is too subtle it will lose all form and structure once it is on the floor.

Tone in design

The tone of a colour depends on the amount of black there is in the colour. The blacker the colour, the darker the tone and the less black, the lighter the tone. A tone scale would show the range from black, through dark greys, middle greys and light greys to white.

If tone is to be used as a major design element, there are a number of ways that this can be done. You may wish to work only in a tone range in one colour, that is, in monochrome. This may be from black to white, but the same principle applies also to the use of any other single colour. The tones that you chose may stretch across the whole range, or can be limited to a shortened series, which may be nearer the lighter end of the scale, in the middle, or limited to the dark tones only.

Detail of sampler showing use of mixed yarns *Roger Oates*

When deciding whether you want your design to be mainly dark or light, you must remember that the situation of the rug will influence this. A dark rug on a light floor will show as a dark shape and will be clearly seen, whereas a light rug on a light floor will blend in with the background, and be seen mainly as an area of texture. This idea can be exploited. You may, for instance, want to make a rug with a border round a centre motif, which could be dark on light, or light on dark. This means that, through the use of the tone alone, the border can be made to be an important visual edge or limit to the design, or can become a means of fading the rug visually into the background.

The appearance of a pattern can be altered completely by changing the tone arrangement in the pattern. When the tone value of a particular area is adjusted, the visual importance is altered. A light shape will stand out if seen against a dark background, show less if against a

Two examples of jute tufting
Susan Bridge

middle tone background, and hardly be seen if put next to a near tone. So you see, with this one idea, there are limitless design possibilities with which you can experiment.

Optical illusion will also affect the visual weight of the pattern, depending on the use of the extreme tones, (near black and near white). A white square on a black background will appear bigger than the same size black square on a white background. If similar size motifs in tone counterchange are to be used, this must be taken into account and adjustments made if they are to be visually the same size.

Tone can also be used to produce a secondary design when used in the pattern combination of shape with shape. It can make verticals, diagonals, horizontals or spot motifs.

The same principles of tone are true when applied to the use of more than one colour. The design possibilities immediately become greater because more than one colour can now be used in the same tone. This means that a given area can be made very much richer in colour content but still have the same weight in the balance of the whole design.

In weaving, the tones can be the tone of an individual yarn when used in mass, or can be achieved by mixing the yarn in the weft, putting varying amounts of different yarn through the shed in each pick. In this way, the tone value of an area can be blended from light, to middle, to dark.

It is a good idea to weave a sampler in black and white to study the effects of the strong contrast in tone, because the structure of weave produces tones which can be seen from a distance, which are not apparent when viewed closely. It is so easy to weave something which looks ideal while still on the loom and yet, when seen from a distance in its proper place, seems to lose much of its perfection. By making a sampler and by working out your pattern in different proportions and on different scales, the way in which black, white and grey affect each other can be studied.

Texture in design

The texture is the surface quality of the rug and it should have both visual and tactile interest. Texture can be achieved through the construction (the weave), by adding threads to the surface of the rug and by the types of yarn used in the making of the rug.

Construction Knotted or tufted rugs have the most obvious tactile qualities. They can have short or long pile, short and long pile combined in one rug or cut and uncut tufts.

Tufts can be made of the same type of yarn or of dissimilar yarns; they can be woven in an all-over pattern or only in certain places; they can be woven to lie in one direction only or in several directions. Pulling out loops will also produce a different surface quality and these can be long, short, with a low twist, with a high twist, densely packed or scattered.

Adding to the surface of the rug Soumak can provide added texture in horizontal, vertical and diagonal lines. It can be of varying thicknesses and in all-over or block pattern.

Types of yarn The quality of the weft yarn itself will alter both the look and the feel of the rug. Yarn can be shiny, matt, soft, rough, smooth, slippery, hairy, crêpey, thick or thin, and yarns of the same colour, but in different textures, can be used very imaginatively and to great effect.

Twisted wefts *Ann Croot*

Using colour

In designing, colour is a very important factor. It can alter the mood of a pattern by being bright and sunny, or rich and subdued. It can be used in graded bands to form pattern, or be used strategically to add jewel-like areas.

The primary colours

The three primary colours are yellow, cyan (blue) and magenta. The secondary colours are made by mixing yellow and cyan to make green, cyan and magenta to make violet, and magenta and yellow to make orange. The colour circle (Fig. 85, page 64) shows the movement from one colour to another around the circle. The complementary colours are yellow and violet, red and green, and cyan and orange.

Complementary colours appear to make each other more brilliant if they are used together, so a small amount of an opposing colour can be added to an area to increase the impact of a colour.

In weaving, it is possible to get very rich and vibrant colours because more than one coloured yarn can be used together in the weft. If four wefts are being used as one they can be in mixtures of 1/3, 2/2, 3/1 of two colours, 4 single colours or 2/1/1 of three colours.

If the colours chosen are in the same range of colour, ie all reds, or red to orange, the richness of the red will be increased because the colours will mix together to make a brighter shade.

Random pattern in twisted weft technique

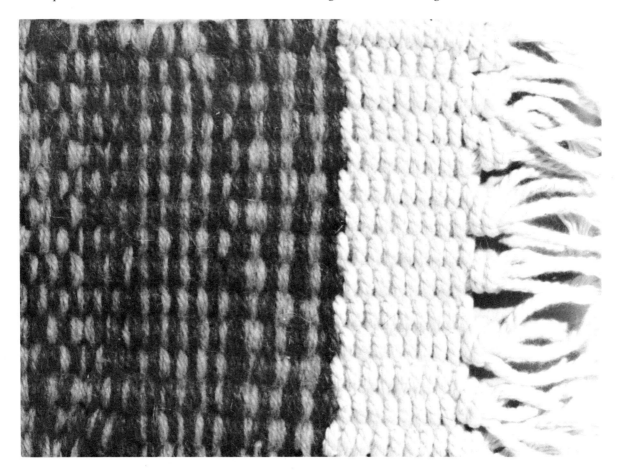

Care must be taken, however, if near primary colours are used in small proportions because they will blend and produce a brownish or greyish colour at a distance.

The mixing of wefts in varying amounts is a very useful technique because the weight of the pattern can be altered by means of colour and a much softer edge can be given to the joining colour zones.

The mixing of yarns is particularly relevant when using knotting techniques; as more threads are used to each tuft, very subtle changes can be made.

In tapestry weave, if all the wefts are mixed and a pattern is being woven, the result will be messy. It is better to use mixed wefts next to an area of unmixed yarn, for contrast.

More ways with colour and patterns Colour can also be used to form a pattern in the weft by twisting two wefts together in one shed, forming a design that is not ordered by any lifting or warp ends, but is made in a plain weave plan. This is called twisted weft technique.

Twisted weft technique If two wefts of different colour are put together through one shed it is possible to make patterns by altering the order in which they lie and by twisting them to make diagonals of different thickness, diamonds and blocks, as well as vertical lines.

Using black and white:

1. To make spots, put the black and white wefts through the shed so that the black lies nearest the woven part of the rug. On the next row, put the two colours through the shed in the same order so that the black is next to the white in the previous row (Fig. 86).

2. To make horizontal lines, put the black and white wefts through the shed so that the black lies nearest the woven part of the rug. On the next row put the colours through the shed so that the white weft lies

Fig. 86: *Twisted weft: spots and horizontal stripes.*

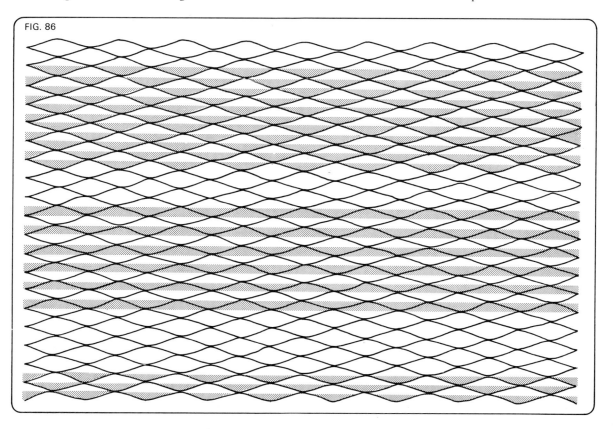

FIG. 86

nearest the white in the previous row. If this order is repeated, thin horizontal lines will be made by the top and bottom halves of the adjacent wefts (Fig. 86).

To change the pattern in a particular area or to make diagonals, diamonds, blocks or vertical lines, the black and white wefts are put through the shed and then twisted in a certain manner.

To make a diagonal join between a spotted area and a striped area

Working from the right, put the black and white through the shed so that the black lies at the bottom, (nearest the weaving). On the next row put the black and white through in the same order and then twist the white downwards so that the white crosses the black on top of *one* of the warp ends and continues across with the white now at the bottom, (nearest the weaving). Repeat these two rows, moving the position of the twist once to the left each time (Fig. 87).

White, black, white diagonal on a spotted ground

Working from the left, put the black and white through so that the white is at the bottom. Twist these upwards three times so that there is first white, then black, then white lying on top over three adjacent warp ends (the weft continues across with the white now above the black in the shed).

Working from the right, put the wefts through so that the black lies at the bottom. Twist the wefts three times downwards so that there is first white, then black, then white lying over the top of the next three

Fig. 87 : *Twisted wefts; one spot diagonal between two areas, one with stripes, the other with spots.*
Fig. 88 : *Twisted wefts; 2/1 diagonal between two areas of spots.*

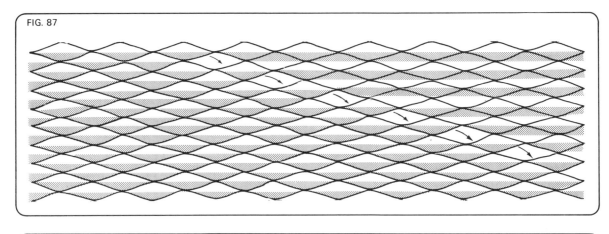

FIG. 87

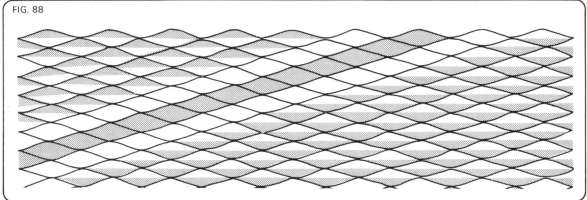

FIG. 88

diagonal warp ends. Repeat these two rows to make the diagonal. The spots on one side of the diagonal will have black at the top and the spots on the other side will have white at the top (Fig. 88).

Diagonals in two colours on a striped background
Working from the left with black on the top in the weft, twist the wefts twice so that there is first black and then white lying on top over two adjacent warp ends (black will continue across the weft on top). Working from the right with white on top, twist the wefts twice downwards so that there is first white and then black on the surface over the next two adjacent warp ends in the warp, (white will continue across the weft on top). Repeat these two rows moving diagonally each time when twisting to form the pattern (Fig. 89).

Vertical stripes in two colours on a striped background
Working from the right with white on top in the weft, make two black and white vertical stripes nine warp ends apart. Twist these twice downwards so that white is uppermost over the outer ends in the black (1 and 9), and then twist the wefts again so that the inner ends have black uppermost (3 and 7). Working from the left, put the wefts through with black on top.

Repeat these two rows, working so that the same ends are used for the twist each time – first 1 and 9, then 3 and 7, so that the lines are built up vertically. The wefts are twisted downwards together for each twist so that two twists are made in each movement (Fig. 90).

Fig. 89: *Twisted weft; diagonals in two colours on a striped background.*
Fig. 90: *Twisted weft; vertical stripes in two colours on a striped background.*

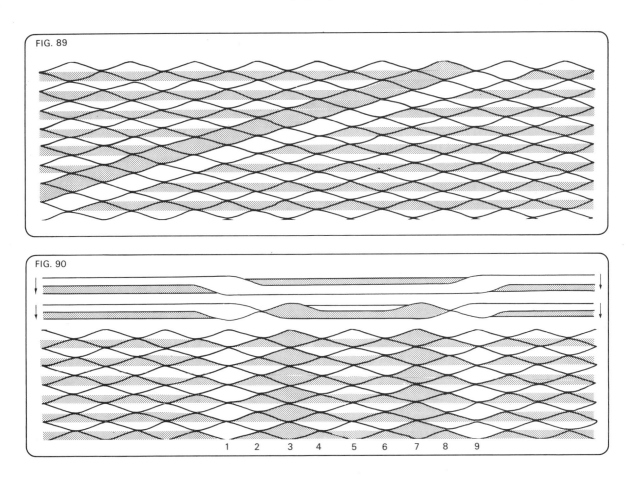

Suppliers

Suppliers of weaving equipment
Dryads Handicrafts Ltd., Northgates, Leicester, England.
Looms, shuttles, skein winders, warping pegs and mills, loom-cord.

K. Drummond, 30 Hart Grove, London W5, England.
Wooden ski shuttles.

John Maxwell, Folders Lane, Burgess Hill, Sussex, England.
Strong, well-made handlooms to standard or individual specifications.

Suppliers of warp yarns
Dryads Handicrafts Ltd., Northgates, Leicester, England.
Cotton and flax yarn.

H. & J. Jones, 58 Wood Street, Liverpool, England.
Good range of soft spun cotton yarns, also hemp, jute, ramie yarns of various plies. Unspun hemp and jute. Minimum quantity 1lb.

Pymore Mill & Co. Ltd., Bridport, Dorset, England.
Various plies of hemp, jute and cotton yarns and loom-cord.

Suppliers of weft yarns
Borgs, Lund, Sweden.
Suppliers of all types of yarns, including many grades of linen rug warp: Mattgarn, 35 per cent wool, 65 per cent fibres, a single yarn in good colours: Notharsgarn, 100 per cent wool singles yarn; Afghargarn, very high quality lustrous worsted for rya rugs; Frostagarn, more normal quality for rya rugs in many colours.

Craftsmen Mark Yarns, Broadlands, Shortheath, Farnham, Surrey, England.
A range of yarns specially spun for handweavers. Includes a 2-ply rug wool in white, natural grey and natural black, about 40yds per ounce, also 6/10s lea linen rug warp. Minimum quantity 1lb.

A. K. Graupner, Corner House, 4 Valley Road, Bradford 1, England.
2-ply rug wool.

W. Morgan & Son, Wallis Factory, Ambleston, Haverfordwest, Wales.
Single and 2-ply rug wools in natural greys. Minimum quantity 4lb. Yarns specially dyed in amounts not less than 30lbs.

Weavers' Shop, Royal Carpet Factory, Wilton, nr. Salisbury, Wilts, England.
A good range of 2/55s carpet wool in white and dyed colours. Also a 6-ply yarn, minimum quantity ½lb. Wool can be specially dyed if not less than 12lbs of one colour is required. Small charge for samples.

Suppliers in America

Magnolia Weaving, 2635 29th West, Seattle, Washington 98199.
A weavers' supply house that has cotton, wool, jute.

Mrs. Lyle B. Robinson, 1019 N.E. 62nd, Seattle, Washington 98115.
A weavers' supply house.

Troy Yarn and Textile Company, Pawtucket, Rhode Island 02860.
A weavers' supply house that is an excellent source for wool rug yarns.

Williams and Company, Box 318, Madison Square Station, New York,
New York 10010.
A weavers' supply house that specialises in linen yarns.

The Yarn Depot, 545 Sutter Street, San Francisco, California 94102.
*A weavers' supply house that carries cotton, jute and wool yarns that come
in exciting colours.*

Bibliography

Beutlich, Tadek. The Technique of Woven Tapestry.
Batsford. 1967.
Bennett, Ian. Book of Oriental Carpets and Rugs.
Hamlyn. 1972.
Collingwood, Peter. The Techniques of Rug Weaving.
Faber. 1968.
Edwards, Edward B., Pattern and Design with Dynamic Symmetry.
Dover. 1967.
Grierson, Ronald. Woven Rugs.
Dryad.
Meyer, Franz Sales. Handbook of Ornament.
Dover.
Reed, Stanley. Oriental Rugs and Carpets.
Weidenfeld and Nicolson. 1967.
Tovey, John. The Technique of Weaving.
Batsford. 1965.
Audsley, W. & G. Designs and Patterns from Historic Ornament.
Dover.

Index